The
Lambourn Branch
revisited

Kevin Robertson

NOODLE BOOKS

Dedication:
To Ken who suggested it and Bernard who made it all possible.

ISBN 978-1-906419-06-6

First published in 2008 by Kevin Robertson
under the **NOODLE BOOKS** imprint
PO Box 279
Corhampton
SOUTHAMPTON
SO32 3ZX

www.kevinrobertsonbooks.co.uk

Printed in England by the Alden Press

Front cover / Title page - *The typical off-peak Lambourn passenger service of the final years; a single coach and Pannier Tank. Here an unidentified member of the 57xx class has pushed the coach backwards so as to clear the run round loop. On most occasions after re-coupling the train would set back and stand under the canopy to await departure time.*

Colour Rail

Rear cover - *Through the bushes near Speen. 3rd November 1973.*

David Canning

Below - *Supper invitation to Mr John East Penfold of Lambourn. See pages 11 and 21.*

The Penfold Collection

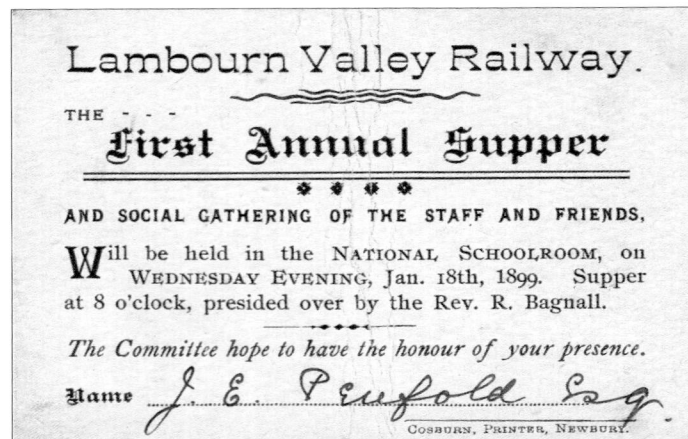

Lambourn Valley Railway.

THE - - -

First Annual Supper

AND SOCIAL GATHERING OF THE STAFF AND FRIENDS,

Will be held in the NATIONAL SCHOOLROOM, on WEDNESDAY EVENING, Jan. 18th, 1899. Supper at 8 o'clock, presided over by the Rev. R. Bagnall.

The Committee hope to have the honour of your presence.

Name *J. E. Penfold Esq*

COSBURN, PRINTER, NEWBURY.

CONTENTS

INTRODUCTION

I have wanted to produce this book for some time. Over 20 years in fact, although at every previous attempt outside circumstances intervened. In consequence it took a chance telephone call and meeting to really push the project along. Indeed, in the summer of 2007 I realised that no more excuses could be made and it was a question of probably now or never.

Having been involved with Roger Simmonds on the original Lambourn Branch book produced in 1984, it inevitably transpired that further material would come to light. Sometimes it was a photograph, at other times a snippet of information, or maybe an artefact paper or otherwise, all competing to be added to the history of what may truly be described as a 'typical Great Western Branch Line'. At this point I expect the purists to stand up and start throwing brick-bats, 'Ah, but the Lambourn line never did this……..and it never carried that……..". Fine, perhaps it did not do everything that would put it in the 'typical' criteria, but what it did do is provide a service to the community for over sixty years, a community which during that time could no more have imagined a valley without trains than we could nowadays visualise one with them.

With time now fast approaching half a century since trains ran to Lambourn, it might be thought there was little left to uncover. I doubt that very much. Any form of research will answer many questions but equally throw up others that were unknown of beforehand.

I have to confess I never travelled on the Lambourn line nor, indeed, saw it in operation although I did come close. Back in 1971 I recall writing to British Railways enquiring over the possibility of a trip in the brake van of a goods train from Newbury over the then extent of the route to Welford Park. This was approved, but subject to the sum of £5.00 being paid, no doubt to cover the wages of an Inspector who would have to accompany me. Regretfully I declined. As a poor and impoverished student I could ill afford such an amount. Nowadays I would willingly pay that £5.00, perhaps even a little more, should that opportunity still be available. Of course it never will be. Later, I also missed the chance to travel on the 1973 specials. Not living in the area at the time meant I was unaware until later that the event had even occurred. C'est la vie.

This book is not intended to be a re-run of history, neither have I attempted to distil the same facts in a different form. Instead it is a new, more personal approach, which I trust will have a wider appeal, to the enthusiast of course and also to the local community.

All I can hope is that, in consequence of this latest attempt, a few more facts, features and even funnies relevant to the railway may be revealed. If those of you reading this book gain as much pleasure from its pages as I have had in their compilation then the exercise will certainly have been worthwhile.

Kevin Robertson

East Garston was renowned for its floral display, the work of Tom Liddiard, Porter-in-Charge. He is seen here with some examples of his handiwork and also it is believed, the Lever sisters.   *Hilary Reem*

ACKNOWLEDGEMENTS

As mentioned opposite, the present work owes much to two people. Ken Tarbox from East Garston who set up and runs the Lambourn Valley Railway website www.kentarbox.com/images/ lambourn-valley-railway - well worth a visit as well, and also Bernard Smith, former Welford Park signalman and, as will be gathered from some of the illustrations, is a definite motor cycle enthusiast as well.

Ken and I first spoke following my discovery of his web-site, which, thanks to the medium of the worldwide-web, has attracted visitors and interest in the Lambourn line from a far greater area than was possible by mere foot slogging 25 years ago. Ken had also been approached by a third party who suggested there was a retired Welford Park signalman living in Newbury who had never been spoken to before, that man of course was Bernard.

There followed several enjoyable evenings spent at local hostelries as well as suggestions from Bernard as to who to contact next. Accordingly I was fortunate to meet Bernard's former signalman colleague from Welford Park, Charlie Marshall and also Roy Flitter who started his own career as a Lad Porter at Speen.

Listening to these men was like being transported back to another age. An age in which I was a child, at that time not living far from the railway but never, regretfully, travelling upon it. It also made me realise how little I did know and, consequently, whilst much of the present text has been shown to Bernard in advance for the purpose of checking, I trust that my interpretation of the various reminiscences have been correct. Any errors that remain, however, are mine alone. To Charlie Marshall also I owe an especial debt of gratitude. He had never seen me before and yet without question he willingly loaned me a wallet of photographs he had taken, a priceless record.

More recently, others having come to hear of the project have also been generous in their encouragement and assistance. Peter Penfold (not forgetting Siobhan of course), for allowing access to The Penfold Collection - every time I thought we were finished another note would arrive, "I've found some more...". Cecil Rackham, David Rosier, Pat Legg, Graham Pearson and David Pottinger. The latter's permission to included the drawings from his late Father have enabled the story to be truly completed. Also at what was literally the eleventh hour, to Frank Dumbleton of the Great Western Society. To these persons I owe much.

Sadly, so many others who assisted in the original book are no longer around. But whilst their names may therefore not thus appear here, they are still appreciated. Without their help none of this would have been possible.

I hope also that most of the photographs will be newly seen as well. Unfortunately, as is often the case, some photographs, loaned, purchased, acquired etc, do not have annotation details on the reverse and therefore it is impossible to correctly ascertain any copyright. My sincere apologies for any error in this area.

Amongst new friends who have assisted , I must also thank Bruce Murray for his guidance with photographs. Similarly Peter Bailey, whose guiding hand and copious use of red pen and pencil on the various drafts are ever appreciated.

Finally I feel a definite debt of gratitude is owed to the man who might almost be said to be the founder, certainly the saviour of the railway in its earliest years, Col J A Archer-Houblon. Had he not the foresight to pursue the goal of a railway through the valley, a century later this book could not have been written.

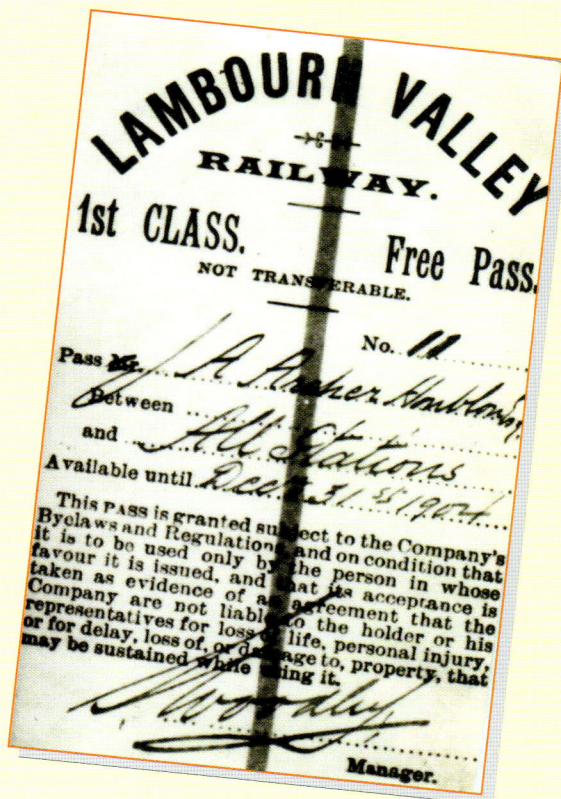

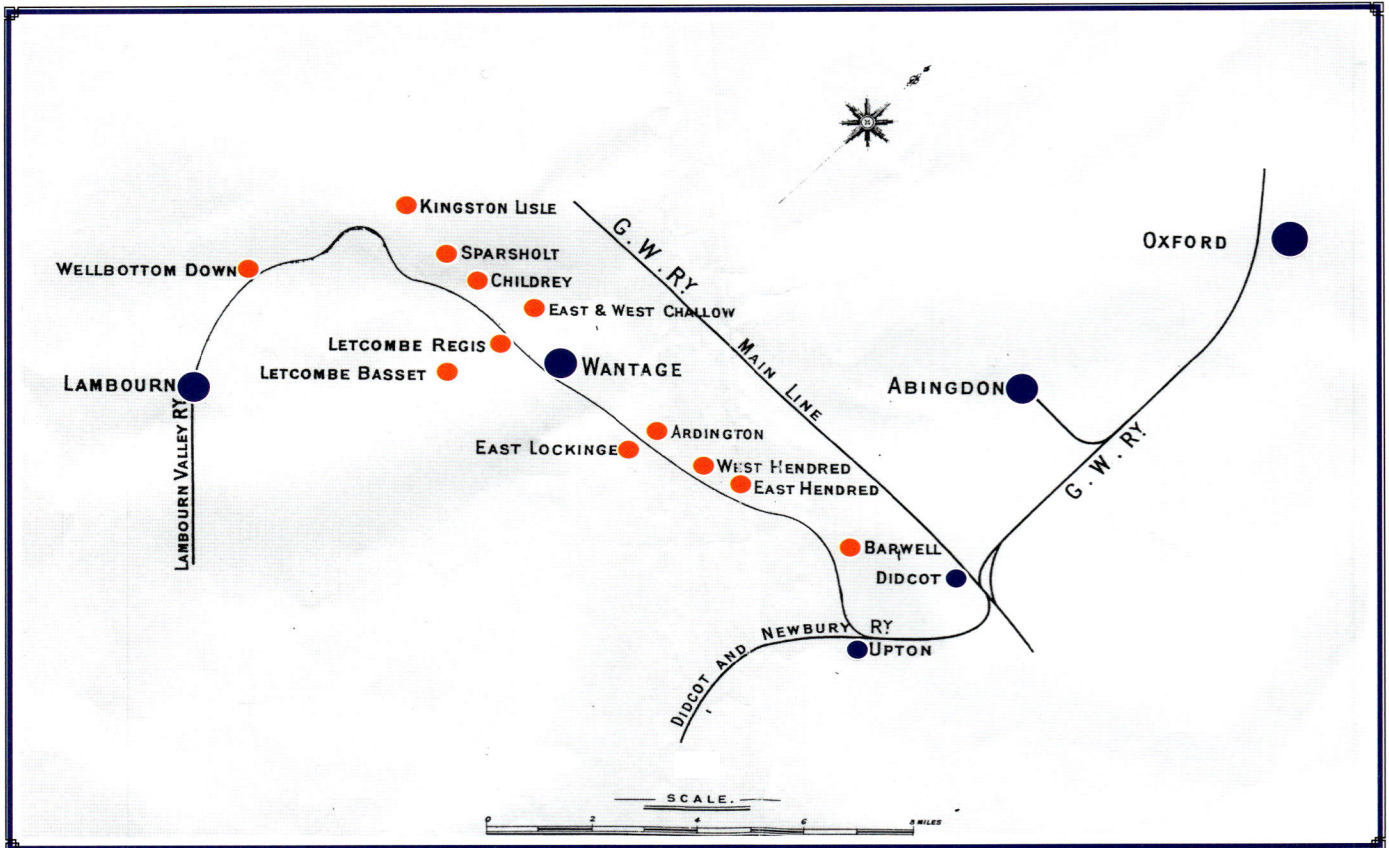

The Chance of Expansion

In 1899 a proposal was mooted for an expansion of the railway from Lambourn through the villages of what was then north Berkshire, to connect into the erstwhile independent Didcot, Newbury and Southampton Railway, near to that routes own station at Upton (- later Upton and Blewbury.) The promoter for this 17½ mile route was a Captain C H Bingham,

The intended line would be built as a Light Railway under the 1896 Act and thus would obtain certain benefits relative to operating costs, although in consequence it would be restricted as to the speed trains would be able to achieve.

The proposal was sent to Mr W H H M Gipps, who shared the roles of General Manager of the Lambourn Valley Railway and Traffic Manager of the Didcot, Newbury & Southampton. Apart from this commonality, the two lines had no connection, geographically or in business terms.

Capt Bingham estimated the route could be built for just £5,000 per mile, although he was evidently unaware of the precarious financial situations affecting both concerns. For this and other reasons Gipps did not recommend that his respective Boards pursue the plan and nothing else is heard of it. (Interesting to relate, to consider a 17½ mile extension would have been far longer than the length of actual LVR itself.)

It may be worthwhile to consider for a moment how Captain Bingham may have seriously thought the venture worthwhile. Even over a century later the area to be traversed is rural in the extreme. There would have been little opportunity then for generating extra traffic.

Indeed, the buffers at Lambourn Station would for ever mark the end of the line, no sensible promoter being likely to see expansion as a commercial proposition. (See also note on page 57).

THE INDEPENDENT AND EARLY YEARS

Despite the passage of time since the little Lambourn Valley Railway ceased to exist under the nationalised British Railways network, further information has come to light, principally because of the gathering of former records in what was then the Archive of British Railways Board at Porchester Road, London.

Much of this additional information took the form of brittle papers clipped together, which because of their very fragile state, had not been sent to what was then known as the Public Record Office - nowadays the National Archive.

We already know of course the basic facts of the Lambourn Valley Railway. The first proposal for what was then a tramway can be traced back to 1873 but it would be some years before a concrete scheme evolved and work eventually began in 1888. Unfortunately a dispute with the contractor, together with financial difficulties, saw the project stall in 1891, even though it was by that time three-quarters complete. It would remain dormant for a further seven years until eventually completion occurred in 1898.

The railway would remain independent for just seven years, until absorbed by the Great Western, becoming just another example of a local scheme destined to be lost to the larger conglomerate, who in this way also secured a means of expanding its own system at notional cost.

Before 1905, indeed even before the time of opening in 1898, we have new information. Commencing on 15th August 1895 it was recorded that, to accommodate Lambourn trains at Newbury, the cramped station conditions would have to be extended, at an estimated cost of £5,500. This work would be carried out by the GWR themselves, although the LVR had to agree to an interest charge of 3% on the capital outlay together with necessary the costs of maintenance.

Further expense was agreed on 14th February 1896, this time for £60 to connect a water crane at Newbury to accommodate LVR trains. The work was again carried out by GWR, who charged the LVR the same rate of 3%.

Next on 15th May 1897 we have a progress report on completion from the columns of the *NEWBURY WEEKLY NEWS*, "The progress which is being made with the construction of the Lambourn Railway is very gratifying and Newbury people evince their interest in the proceedings by making the line a favourite promenade on Sunday afternoons. The view to be gained from the embankment across the Moors is a very pleasant one. The Kennet winding its circuitous way through the green meadows, the trees of Speen on one side, with the red topped tower peeping through the woods of Hampstead on the other, and the hills of Hampshire bounding the distant horizon. The sun was shining brightly on Sunday, and the river was alive with boating parties and the line with promenaders. The Moors, which once were deserted, save by the moor-hen, the dabchick and the water rat, presented a lively aspect, and plainly indicated the advance of civilisation."

What comes next is a clear indication that, even though completion and opening were but a few months away, no definite conclusion appears to have been made as to who would be operating the railway. The route was, of course, being completed by the LVR themselves, although up to this time there was no record of where locomotives might be sourced from. Curiously, the LVR records do not at this stage allude to this point and instead we have a note from the General Manager of the GWR at Paddington to the GWR's Chief Mechanical Engineer of 2nd July 1897, in which a rather curious figure of £60 is mentioned should the GWR be requested to work the route. Evidently the GWR was similarly unsure of the likely future arrangements as the note concludes that, should the LVR use their own engines and require water to be taken at Newbury, this would be

A remarkable photograph taken inside a train on the Lambourn line in 1946. The passenger is Mr K W Kibblewhite Pounds, then aged 80 and who resided for the whole of his life at Lone Barn.
Mr Kibblewhite Pounds worked first as a carpenter and wheelwright, his father's trade, and then as a farmer. He served on the East Garston parish council from its formation in 1894 until the late 1940s, for several years as its chairman.

Colin Pounds

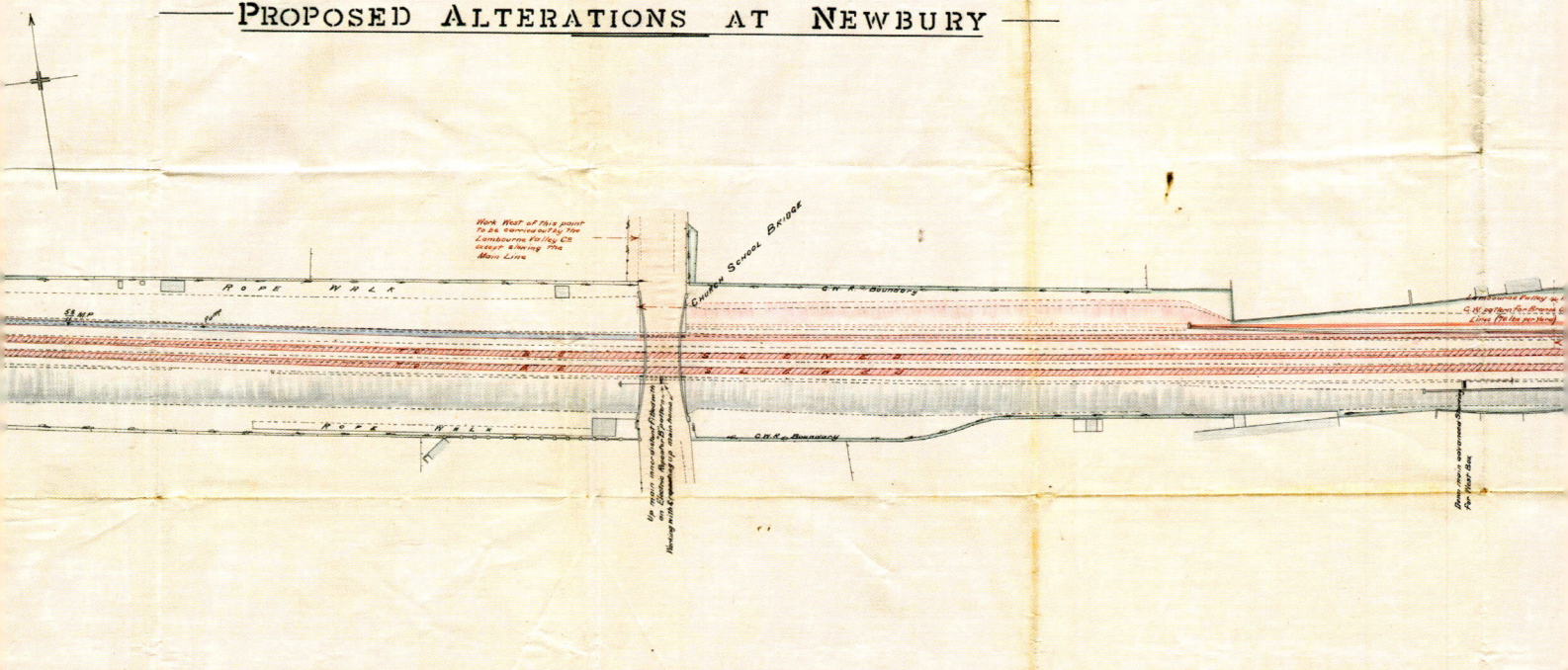

Early days at Newbury and the plan which accompanied the October 1897 Agreement between the LVR and GWR concerning the use of the station. (The original drawing continued westwards for some distance, to the point where the branch diverged. Interestingly, at this point a distant signal is shown, warning approaching trains of the approach to the station, which is referred to as having an electric repeater of 'Type B'. The type referred to is unknown, but even so and bearing in mind the date, this must have been one of the earliest installations of an electrical repeater for a signal.)

The main Berks and Hants line is also seen, coloured red, which indicated where the main line would need to be slewed south in order to afford sufficient space for the new single line alongside it. Whilst the LVR were responsible for their work west of Church Street Bridge, everything east of the bridge and the actual slewing was undertaken by the GWR - and no doubt charged to the LVR accordingly. A note, referring to the up inner distant signal, located on the main line by the bridge, again refers to the same type of repeater being fitted.

Moving east, Black Boys Bridge comes next, with another note beside this to the effect that from here on the LVR was fitted with standard 'GWR Branch Permanent-way', the rail weighing 76 lbs per yard.

Further east still, it is just possible to identify the ordinal layout at the west end of Newbury station, which clearly included a siding where the bay was now to be placed. (See inset).

The Lambourn line's connection with the main line can also be seen, including the location of the 9-lever ground frame working the various signals, points and facing point locks.

The track and signalling layout may also be worthy of mention, as the only two semaphore signals applicable to the LVR were both on the same post, respectively an 'Up Branch Home' and 'Down Branch Starting'. Thus no semaphore signals are shown allowing direct access to or from the branch. It would appear that even at this early stage, through running was not considered.

There were two loops applicable to the LVR the first for obvious reasons alongside the bay platform, whilst the second was between the up main line and branch running line. This could well have been intended for the exchange of freight, the exit points being locked by a key on the train staff and the actual points, if not protected by point-discs, operated with their associated independent discs from the Ground Frame.

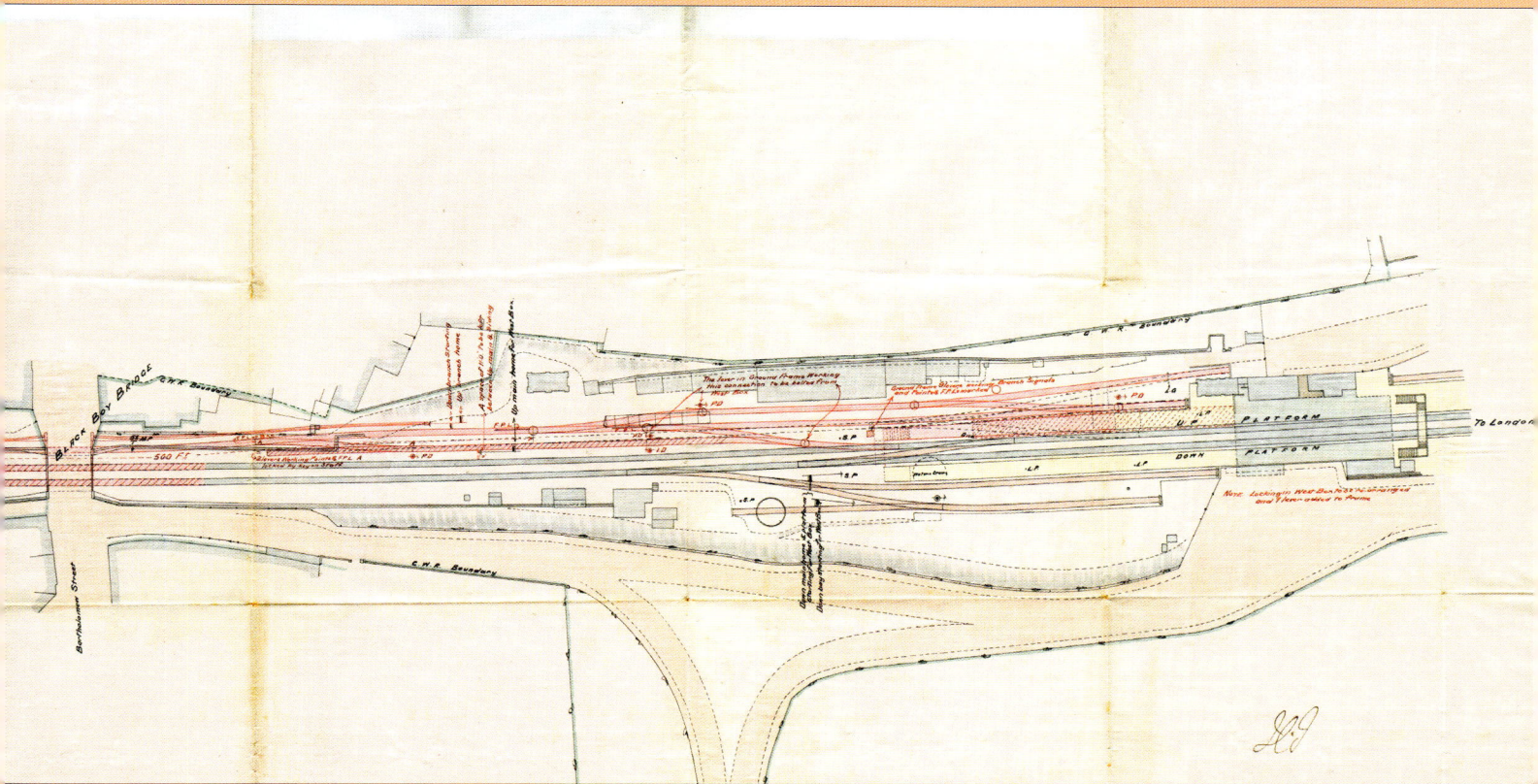

Newbury of course, was at this time just provided with up and down platform roads under an overall roof. It would later be rebuilt in the form which basically survives today at the expense of the Didcot, Newbury & Southampton Company, whose few DNS trains could hardly have made much difference to the working at the station. However, the GWR, as astute as ever, had also been upgrading the Berks and Hants generally, both locally and further west, to provide a more direct route to the West Country. Therefore Newbury did indeed need some form of expansion. What better way then than to get the DNS to pay for the work as indeed they did - but that is another story.

Returning to the plan above, the small turntable will also be noted, this would disappear later.

The cost to the Lambourn Valley Co. for use of the new facilities at Newbury was £50 pa, payable to the GWR with the right to commute this to a one off payment of £1,000 if desired. Not surprisingly, this option was never undertaken.

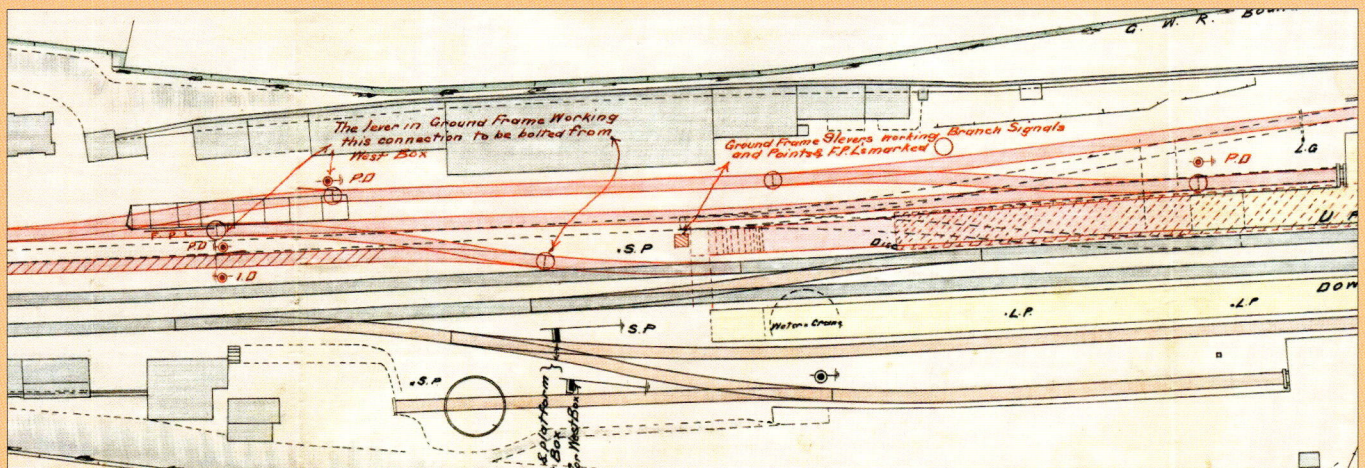

LAMBOURN VALLEY RAILWAY.

The Chairman and Directors

Of The Lambourn Valley Railway Company

Request the pleasure of

Mr J. E. Antobus'   Company

At the Public Opening of the Line

On Saturday, April 2nd, 1898, leaving Newbury

Station at 11.0 a.m.

R.S.V.P.
To General Manager,
    Lambourn Valley Railway,
        11, Oxford Street, Southampton.

The Opening of the Lambourn Valley Railway, Saturday 2nd April 1898

Opposite is a similar, but certainly not the same illustration as appeared in the original work. Comparing the two, there are fewer people to be seen and this may well mean the view was taken during the period the official party were touring the town prior to the special returning to Newbury at 1.00 pm. Below the view is an original initiation made out to Mr John East Penfold, who together with his wife, Louisa, ran the Red Lion Hotel in Lambourn. (See also pages 20 / 21) Mr John East Penfold also held two shares in the railway and this may well explain his invitation, although another reason was that he was also the first chairman of the Lambourn Parish Council, having been elected to the role in 1896. Of course as the invitation referred to the 11.00 am from Newbury, this would mean he would presumably have had to make his own way to Newbury - travel to Lambourn on the special - return again by train to Newbury and then make his own way back again! (Public services did not start until Monday 4th April). Just a few years later, Mrs Louisa Penfold at the Red Lion would be involved in providing teas to visitors travelling by rail excursion. (See pages 20 / 21).

It is believed the photograph may have been one of a series taken by a local photographer whose work had included recording scenes of the Lambourn area on the large glass plates of the period. Some years later these plates were purchased, wiped clean and used for a greenhouse.

A contemporary record of the first public working on Monday 4th April, refers to the fact there was so much merrymaking on board, the Guard was unable to collect fares from all the children who were carried.

The Penfold Collection.

Right - The inaugural dinner under the Chairmanship of the then Vicar of Lambourn, Rev. R. Bagnell. It is not believed Rev. Bagnell had any formal position on the railway. The originals of both cards shown were edged in gold leaf. Mr Penfold was one of 70 guests invited to the subsequent luncheon held on the same day.

The location for what can only be described as having been a sumptuous feast is not stated, but by implication this was at the "George" Hotel. This establishment and likewise Mr. Booth, are also referred to on page 20.

The name Penfold is of course just one that was synonymous with Lambourn . Peter Penfold's father John Penfold, was well known within the area having worked as a Clerk at Lambourn between 1939 and 1951, although with a gap for wartime Naval service. After leaving the railway, John Penfold moved to work at the new facility at Harwell. This was around the same time, 1951, that Harry Knapp, the son of the last Station Master at Lambourn, Stan Knapp and who is referred to several times in the final chapter, also left the railway to likewise move to Harwell.

Lambourn Valley Railway.

INAUGURAL DINNER,

WEDNESDAY, JANUARY 18TH, 1899.

Chairman .. .. REV. R. BAGNALL.

Menu.

Turkey.   Sausages.

Roast Chicken and Bacon.

Ducks.

Veal and Ham.

Boiled Beef.   Roast Beef.

Boiled Leg of Mutton.   Roast Leg of Mutton.

Steak and Kidney Pies.

Veal and Ham Pies.   Rabbit Pies.

Plum Puddings.   Mince Pies.

Apple Pies.

Jellies.   Pastry.

Cheese and Celery.

W. S. BOOTH,
Caterer,
"GEORGE" HOTEL,
LAMBOURN.

COSBURN. PRINTER. NEWBURY.

A stunning rendition of the original station at Lambourn soon after opening in 1898. It is not possible to identify many of those present with any certainty, although those furthest to the right must certainly be a locomotive crew. Second in from the left is the Station Master, Mr. W. Brain and who as the senior member of operational staff on the line, also acted as Traffic Manager. (Mr Brain also appears to have been what would nowadays be referred to as a property developer, as around 1900 he was responsible for the buildings of several substantial houses in the Lambourn Valley, including Station Houses in Bockhampton Road, he lived at No.2. A number of these properties are still standing). As was customary for the period, a number of enamel signs are seen, including one for 'Freeman, Hardy, Willis - Boots & Shoes', there is also a sweetmeat machine, probably dispensing chocolate. Notice also the poster board with the heading 'Lambourn Valley' attached to which is what is probably a timetable poster. In the immediate foreground is the pit for the engine shed., the latter structure was later extended so that the pit was wholly within the building. The light section trackwork is apparent. The station survived basically in this form until take over by the Great Western. The main building was then demolished although the dark coloured hut - at the time it was recorded here its use is not known, was retained on the new raised platform, see top drawing page 123. Mr Brain has fortunately left some comments as to the traffic handled and capabilities of the LVR's own locomotives. When these arrived, he stated they were able to take 20 loaded wagons to Newbury, compared with just 6 behind the engine(s) first hired by the GWR. Similarly in 1899 he referred that upwards of 2,000 horses had been carried by January 1899 whilst passengers numbers amounted to 9,000 persons in the 'holiday period".

The Penfold Collection.

charged to the LVR at the rate of 6d per tank filling.

Nothing else is now heard of until April 1898. We know the line opened on 2nd, initially with a locomotive hired from the GWR. Then, on 16th April, there is a note on the file to the effect that the Newbury water crane, referred to earlier, had been superseded by a four-inch standpipe. Further comment concerning the water supply at Newbury continued, although the eventual conclusions are not totally clear. What can be said with certainty is that the GWR supplied the water at Newbury and charged the LVR for it. Consequently the LVR would fill their engines at Lambourn whenever possible and save an unnecessary cost!

Based on figures prepared by the accountants office at Swindon, we then have some very useful detail that is deduced from the water consumption figures ,although this time informing on the number of trains actually run. This commences on 28th March 1899 when the line had been open just a few days short of one year. We are told the railway was making six return journeys per day in summer and five at other times, except for six again on Saturdays. In addition to this there were a number of special workings on Saturdays.

2nd April 1898 to 26th March 1899	
Ordinary trains - Weekdays	1,738
Special trains - Weekdays	28
Special trains - Sundays	55
Total	**1,821 ***

* Clearly maths was different in 1898 as the total shown on the original letter was 1,831 whilst underneath it has been corrected by another unknown hand to 1,826!

Whilst it may appear trivial to continue on the theme of water supplies, it is from these records that so much new information has been uncovered. For example, the LVR were originally charged 3d per tank of water from Newbury, but following representations by the LVR to the GWR, a memo was sent signed by none other than G J Churchward who agreed to a 50% reduction in the charge with effect from 3rd April 1899.

Next comes another memorandum, this time from the Accountants Office at Paddington to William Dean at Swindon. Dated 4th May 1899, it states, "...I have communicated with the Lambourn Valley Company who, as you know, are not in very good financial circumstances. They now admit that the agreement giving them the use of Newbury Station without charge for five years after the opening of their line, does not apply to water for their engines......... . They point out, which is a fact, that they have to pay interest on the outlay at Newbury for their accommodation, including the Water Column through which their engines are supplied with water, and further state that their engines do not take more than 150 gallons at a time. They ask that under these circumstances they may be charged with only the actual cost of the water, including of

Extracts from *THE NEWBURY WEEKLY NEWS*

On 24th March 1898, less than a week before the opening, *The Newbury Weekly News* reported the tragic death of 16 year old Alfred Henry Martin of Wickham Heath, run over by a train at Speen. Alfred was employed to work on the contractors engine, 'Ernest', which had arrived at Speen around 1.00 p.m. from Newbury, coupled to some wagons. In its contemporary description of the accident, the 'NWN' unintentionally provides information of a siding and 'Engine House' at Speen, located just beyond the level crossing, Alfred Martin had run forward to change the points to allow his train to be shunted clear of the 'main line'. Sadly it was then that he tripped over the rails and was run over.

This siding was clearly not retained after opening and it was never mentioned in the subsequent Board of Trade Inspection Report of a week later on 31st March. The locomotive 'Ernest' was also removed by the contractors very shortly afterwards.

A further snippet from the construction concerns a pigsty near East Garston, set on fire by a spark from the contractors engine. After this occurred, the owner would never go to bed until the last train had passed.

A later report from the newspaper commenting upon the Annual General Meeting of the LVR Co in 1899, referred to a suggestion for a siding at Eastbury. As is known, this was never acted upon.

course the repairs to the appliance and suggest 1d per tank instead of 3d." (It would appear this slightly contradicted the earlier note dealt with by Churchward and possibly Paddington were unaware of the latter's contents.) An outcome is not recorded.

We now move forward some five years to 1904, during with period the LVR had first been operating services using their own locomotives and rolling stock although it is indeed possible that goods coming in from some distance and similarly goods out, destined for destinations beyond Newbury, would have used other companies - mainly GWR - vehicles. To state otherwise would imply continual trans-shipment at Newbury which hardly seems feasible.

Again the former Swindon records concerning water supplied at Newbury to LVR engines working make for interesting reading. A memorandum of 21st July 1904 refers to the following 'fills' made in the first five months of the year:

1904	
January	135
February	132
March	145
April	132
May	72
Total	**616**

(The maths are also accurate this time!)

Interestingly, an appended note states this did not include water taken by engines sent from Swindon to work the goods traffic since the introduction of the 'Motor Cars' - sic. (Steam rail-motors.) We will be discussing the early days of the steam rail-motors very shortly, although suffice it to say for now, that it would appear any water taken at Newbury by engines operating the goods services would appear not to have been charged. The type of engines hired from Swindon is also not known for certain, although they would certainly have been of the lightest weight, due to the condition of the LVR as built.

As mentioned in the original book on the line, steam rail-motors were introduced for passenger services in May 1904. As these vehicles were in themselves heavier than the existing rolling stock permitted, a revised inspection was also necessary from the Board of Trade. Reading the detail of this inspection over a century later, a wealth of information is revealed relative, not only to the actual task in hand, but also to the railway. Accordingly it is well worth recounting, not only this detail in full, but also the record of the GWR trials that took place earlier. Possibly the latter was a slightly unusual form of behaviour, but if anything it again confirms the seemingly good relations maintained between the Great Western and Lambourn companies, not withstanding the fact that Paddington had already made at least two approaches to take over the little line and been rebuffed on both occasions.

Firstly it appears the GWR had set some ground rules, as on 12th January 1905 there is a note from an un-named individual at Swindon that any water supplied to the 'Motor-Cars' (it will likewise be noted several different terms are used to describe the vehicles) will be at the same rate as that as that supplied to the engines., viz 1½d per tank. The 1899 reduction then evidently still applied although it is curious that at this stage hired locomotives supplied by Swindon for working the goods traffic were not charged for water whereas the rail-motors were.

The precursor inspection took place on Monday 4th May 1904 and is detailed from the official Swindon records as follows:

"Memorandum: Lambourn Valley line Inspection.

"No. 2 Car sent from Swindon to Newbury - taken thence onto the Lambourn Line with engine attached in front, and Engineering Inspection Coach in the rear.

"Messrs. Taylor, Dawson, W.H. Williams, and Woodley were present. The Car was subsequently sent to Reading to stable in readiness for the Board of Trade Inspection on the following Saturday.

"The line is 12½ miles long with 8 stations.

"There are 12 Girder Bridges over roads and streams including 1 of four spans over the River Kennet.

"The Rail is 50 lbs per yard, and the road is well ballasted. The ruling gradient is 1 in 60........ .

"The Station Platforms vary from 9" to 12" high and stand only 2" clear of the scroll iron of the car.

"At Lambourn the timber at the edge of the platform had to be cut away to clear.

"At Newbury - the stand-pipe in the Down Bay will have to be moved towards the end of the Platform in order that the Cars may be watered with engine end towards Lambourn.

"At Lambourn - there is a small water tank, at the extreme end of the station but the crane will only water the Cars when they enter Lambourn engine end first but there is a hydrant available in the Engine Shed.

"Engine Shed of corrugated iron - rather longer than one Car.

"Carriage Shed of corrugated iron - rather longer than two cars.

"Rolling Stock - 3 locomotives, 4 carriages & brake van, 15 trucks & brake van.

"One of the engines 'Eadweade' was new last year. Cylinders 13" x 20" x 140 lbs pressure, 6 coupled wheels, 3'6" diameter. Carries 21cwts of coal. - Total weight 25 tons.

"'Aelfred' a similar engine was repaired at Swindon '03.

"The third engine 'Ealhswith' was repaired previously.

"The 'Eadweade' will pull 11 GW loaded minerals or 18 GW empties up incline of 1 in 60 and will shunt 30 GW loaded wagons at Newbury Station.

"An engine will be required to run a goods train on the line and do shunting at Newbury. G.W. engine 1384 - 4 wheel coupled side tank is too light for the work.

"The 'Eadweade' is a very efficient short wheel base engine and will I feel sure be found useful."

Three days later on 7th May Col Yorke from the Board of Trade made his formal inspection and again with some most useful detail included in the report.

Two steam rail-motors were used, Car No 1 being sent direct from Swindon to Newbury, whilst Car No 2 was waiting to take Col Yorke and his party from Reading The two cars, coupled together at Newbury - engine ends together, with an additional Inspection Coach at the rear were used in this fashion 'to test the bridges'. (The purpose of this would be for simple deflection tests under the weight of the vehicles. It must be a question of everlasting regret, that despite what is a wealth of wonderful new information, no photographs appear to have been taken to record the event.) .

Those present for the inspection included, Colonel Yorke, Mr. Grierson, Mr. Morris, Mr. Rendell, Mr. Taylor, Mr. Marillier, Mr. W.H. Williams and the Traffic Manager of the Lambourn Valley line.

The Inspector was evidently fully satisfied that the LVR was up to the standard to be operated by rail-motors and consequently it was reported "...the two cars were returned to Swindon for thorough repair so as to be in readiness to start work on Sunday May 15th when the engines, carriages and trucks then on the line were brought to Swindon for sale."

A note in the GWR file commented, "Now that the cars have been allowed to work on the line there can be no objection to a heavier class of engine such as Wolverhampton shunting - being used for the goods work and shunting."

Signed. W.H. Williams"

Seemingly the Traffic Manager of the LVR did not rate highly, as he is not mentioned by name, whilst the reference to Wolverhampton type shunting engines may be taken to mean the '850' class, which commenced running over the line from this time onwards. (History would repeat itself fifty years later, when discussing a suitable replacement for the MSWJ 2-4-0 and 'Dean Goods' steam types then working the services.)

It may be assumed then that, on or shortly after the 15th May the three LVR engines together with the carriage stock and wagons were moved to Swindon. None would ever return to its original haunts and all would eventually be scrapped.

Whilst the era of services operated by the LVRs own locomotives and coaching stock may have been short, the period operated by the steam-railmotors was destined to be even shorter. Car No 1 is shown as being used on Lambourn Valley services from 14th May to 26th November 1904 and again from 19th February to 4th September 1905. Car No 2 is shown as allocated from 14th May to 29th October 1904, accruing 29,226 miles, and then from 13th January to 16th August 1905, this time covering 38,487 miles. The periods out of service were recorded as having been spent at Swindon Works under repair. Another vehicle, No 10, is known to have worked the line, from 16th August to 2nd September 1905. Then we have vehicle No 19 working between 2nd December 1904 and 16th January 1905, 14,136 miles, and also from 19th January to 1st February 1905. Finally No 21 is shown as working between 29th October 1904 and 9th February 1905 and covering 11,630 miles. Taking the last vehicle and mileage as an arbitrary example and without any allowance for a limited service on Sundays and over the Christmas bank holiday, this meant an average daily mileage of something like 111 miles, meaning in the order of 4½ round trips daily. With a service at the time of between four and five return trips daily - dependent upon the day of the week; one railcar was probably sufficient. With a second car, servicing and additional workings could be covered. It gives some indication of the intensity of working

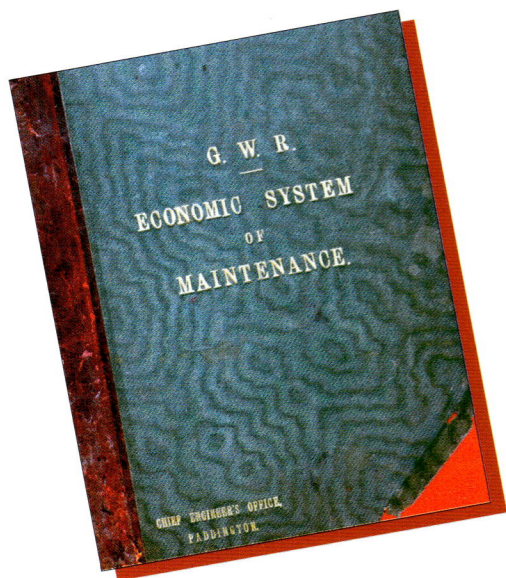

One of the pleasures of undertaking any research is, of course, when new and previously unknown information is uncovered.

Such was the case with the purchase of the book whose cover is seen at the foot of this page. This particular volume had seemingly lain unseen for decades and was unknown of at the time the original Lambourn history was written. The located book described in detail the various GWR lines on which the 'Economic System of Maintenance' (ESM) was installed.

To describe the principals of the 'ESM' fully here would be out of place, although suffice to say many readers will be immediately familiar with its successor the 'Motor Economic System' and associated motorised gangers trolleys.

In both cases the use of a trolley, in the ESM system more accurately described as a hand - pedal powered velocipede, allowed the ganger to inspect a greater section of track than would be possible by just walking.

As can be seen the system was installed on the Lambourn line in 1912, but for an unknown reason was taken out of use just 16 years later.

Removal of the system at this time would also appear slightly strange, especially if it was removed just on the basis of limited usefulness.

Certainly there was no trace of the installation by the 1950s.

Unfortunately, due to the time lapse involved, no one has been found who can recall it in use nor has any recollection from work colleagues suggested why it was indeed abandoned. Just as relevant is the fact that no staff spoken to in connection with the preparation of the original book in 1984, nor with reference to this work, recall motorised gangers trolleys being used on the branch at any time. (Basic push trolleys were used to carry materials a short distance and were in use throughout the system. Indeed one is shown in use at Welford Park in the illustration on page 67. They should not be confused with the ESM system.)

Tantalisingly, in the 1980s and before the existence of the volume referred to was known of, the former GWR / WR collection of photographs became accessible which included a series taken in the 1950s purporting to be of gangers with a motorised inspection car on the Lambourn branch. These views were subsequently shown to several surviving branch staff, but all agreed both the location and men depicted were unknown. It may be concluded that this was a case where the records of the photographic department were inaccurate.

159

Lambourn 12m. 35c.

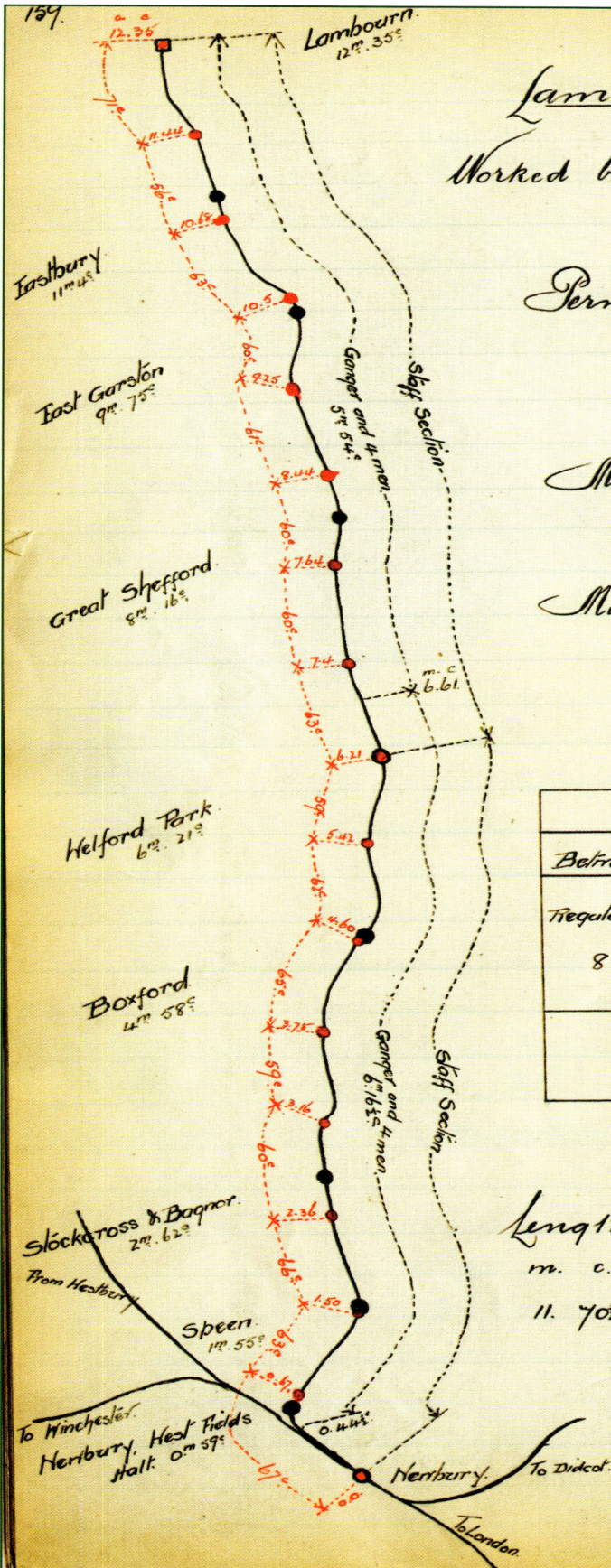

Lambourn Valley Branch.

Worked by Electric Tablet System

Scheme abandoned October. 1928.

Permanent Way.—

Maximum Gradient 1 in

Minimum Curve Radius, chs.

12.35

11.44

10.68

Eastbury 11m. 4c.

10.5

East Garston 9m. 75c.

4.25

Ganger and 4 men. 5m. 54c.

Staff Section

8.44

Great Shefford 8m. 16c.

7.64

7.4

m.c 6.61

6.21

Welford Park 6m. 21c.

5.42

4.60

Boxford 4m. 58c.

3.75

Ganger and 4 men. 3m. 16½c.

Staff Section

3.16

Stockcross & Bagnor 2m. 62c.

2.36

From Hexbury

1.50

Speen 1m. 55c.

0.41

0.44½

To Winchester.

Newbury. West Fields Halt. 0m. 59c.

Newbury. To Didcot.

To London.

No. of Trains.					
Between 6.0 am and 5.30 pm			Per day of 24 hours		
Regular.	Occasional.	Maximum.	Regular.	Occasional.	Maximum.
8	–	8	12	–	12

4 Sunday Trains.

Length.		Double.		Single.		P.W.		Sidings.		Total.	
m.	c.	m.	c.	m.	c.	m.	c.	m.	c.	m.	c.
11.	70½	.	10.	11.	60½	12.	0½	1.	15	13.	15½

Nᵒ of Huts provided with Telephones and
Occupation Key Instruments. — 14.

Nᵒ of Telephones at Stations + Signal Boxes. — 3.

Total. 17

Estimated cost of Installation. —

	£	s.	d.
Telephones and Occupation Key Instruments &c.	300	0	0
14 Telephone Huts.	49	0	0
2 Velocipede Car Huts.	6	0	0
2 Velocipede Cars.	15	0	0
2 Mechanical Trollies.	22	10	0
2 Watches.	4	0	0
2 Suits of Oilskins for Gangers.	1	10	0
Total.	398	0	0

Under Standard Rules this Branch was maintained by. —

	Total Nᵒ of men.	Wages per annum.	Nᵒ of men per mile.
3 Gangs of 4 men ea. =	12.	624. 0. 0.	·91

Under New System. —

2 Gangs of 5 men ea. =	10.	525. 4. 0.	·76
Gross saving in men + wages per ann.	2.	98. 16. 0.	·15

The Gangers are provided with Watches, and examine their own lengths daily on Velocipede Inspection Cars.
Mechanical Trollies are provided for each Gang.

Economic System brought into operation on 23ʳᵈ September, 1913.

Owing to the limited use made of the Economic system, the scheme was abandoned, on this Branch on October, 1928 when the former manning. of 3 Gangs of 4 men each was resorted to. on the 3ʳᵈ December 1928.

required from each vehicle.

All this information, though, immediately raises two questions. Without going into specific days, which readers can work out for themselves from the list above, how, for, example were the services covered during the time the steam rail-motors were not in service? Even more interesting, where were the rail-motors based? Records show the allocation to have been 'Lambourn Valley' and this would imply Lambourn itself, as it is unlikely vehicles would have travelled daily from Swindon. None were shown allocated to Reading at this time.

It was intended that the vehicles would be able to haul a trailing load, some services therefore running as 'mixed' trains. Due to the maximum 1 in 60 gradient on the LVR, the vehicles were supposedly limited to a trailing load of '14 wheels - meaning seven wagons'. However, an official GWR record for 1905 reported that on occasions up to 28 wheels were taken. Possibly one of the reasons for the number of failures that occurred was the extreme demands for steam on occasions.

It took some time to realise that the hard water supply at Lambourn was contributing to some of the steaming problems the vehicles suffered, whilst to be fair the design was seemingly far less reliable generally than a conventional locomotive.

Sadly and no doubt due to the limited period in which they were in operation, no photographs have been located showing a vehicle on the line at this time. The LVR was charged £420 pa for the hire of two vehicles plus the necessary cost of repairs. The latter was likely to have been considerable.

Possibly as a result of the poor performance of the steam-railmotors on the line, the GWR attempted a trial of 'auto-working', details of which are found within a hand written entry in the GWR 'Loco and Carr. Running Dept' minutes Swindon, dated February 15, 1905.

"Trial trip of Trailing car No. 6.

"This car is fitted with gear for working the Regulator on No. 1160 engine so that when it is being propelled the driver can be at the leading end of the Car.
The body is 70 feet in length and is carried on two four wheeled bogies.
"The engine and car were sent from Swindon to Newbury at 8.0 a.m. arriving at the latter station at 10.25 a.m.
"After arrival of the 9.35 a.m. ex Paddington a trial trip was run from Newbury to Lambourn and back - the engine being in front in each direction.
"The car rolled considerably on the Lambourn Valley Line and it was considered not desirable to propel it back to Newbury. On arrival at Newbury the engine was put to the trailing end and the car propelled over the Berks and Hants line to Reading, the engine being driven from the leading end of the car. The car ran very steadily all the way.
"At one point of the road a speed of 40 miles per hour was attained.
"I do not think such a long car suitable for working on the Lambourn Valley Line in its present condition. The steps would have to be raised about 4" as the bottom one does not clear the platforms on the Lambourn Valley Railway.
"I think two hand straps should be put in each of the end compartments the same as those in the large compartments.
"Messrs. Whitelaw, Grierson, Aldington, Louth, Taylor, T.H. Roberts, Marillier, Loco. Inspector Smith and myself accompanied the train.
"Mr. Woodley of the L.V. Line also travelled over the Lambourn Valley section.

Signed. W.H. Waister."

With the number of senior GWR staff on board, was it even a second 'tour of inspection' by the GWR with particular reference to their impending take over of the LVR from the 1st July? Possibly yes, credence being given to this theory by the presence on board of individuals such as Grierson and Aldington. The comment concerning the raising of the steps is also of interest as, if those at the bottom did not clear the platforms, must it mean that there were a number of minor incidents en-route?

With no difficulties experienced in the running of the test train on the main Berks and Hants route, the conclusion must be that the state of the original permanent way on the LVR was poor. Once more such a comment poses further questions. Was this due to limited maintenance or the locomotives which had been used? Could also the railmotors have been responsible? Interestingly No. 1160 referred to above, was a 0-4-2T of the '517' class, with an axle loading in the order of 14 tons, considerably above the maximum 12 tons that had been permitted by the Board of Trade for the steam-railmotor service. It is known that '850' class 0-6-0T engines with an axle load of nearly 11 tons were being used by this time. Perhaps, surprisingly in view of the conclusions drawn, there are no surviving reports of complaints of rough-riding in the early days, although a trip from Newbury to Lambourn in one of the original 4-wheeled coaches complete with wooden seats, is perhaps best left to the imagination!

Takeover of the LVR as an independent company by the GWR took place on the 1st July 1905, shortly after which a permanent revision was made to locomotive hauled trains, both passenger and goods, although, as before some were still classified as 'mixed' workings. This would remain the norm until the advent of the diesel-railcar 30 plus years later.

In consequence of the takeover, the branch was also upgraded throughout between 1905 and about 1910 including the provision of standard Great Western permanent way fittings and presumably an increase in permitted axle loading. It was certainly rated at 12 tons in later years. Presumably also with better track conditions under the GWR, auto-working might well have been reconsidered. Indeed there is suggestion of a further trial involving a 48xx tank and coach sometime in the 1930's, no further information on this has been gleaned.

LAMBOURN VALLEY RAILWAY.

WEEKLY EXCURSIONS

TO

King Alfred's Country,
The Vale of White Horse,
AND
Wayland Smith's Cave,

EVERY MONDAY DURING JULY AND AUGUST.

EXCURSIONS (First and Second Class) will run to LAMBOURN,

The Site of King Alfred the Great's Palace of Lamburna. Lunch will be provided at the George Hotel at Lambourn, and Brakes for the drive, thence over the Berkshire Downs, embracing the site of King Alfred's Palace, Wayland Smith's Cave (celebrated in "Kenilworth"), the famous "Blowing Stone," and White Horse Hill. Afternoon tea will be provided at Lambourn on return, prior to departure of the train for Newbury, London, etc.

Trains leave.					Fares for the Round, including Railway Fare, Cold Lunch, Drive to the White Horse, and Afternoon Tea	
					1st Class. s. d.	2nd Class. s. d.
						13 6
LONDON (Paddington)	} G.W.R.	...	...	9.35 a.m.	18 6	11 6
		...	...	9.5 ,,	15 6	9 0
WINDSOR		...	...	10.30 ,,	11 0	10 3
READING		...	...	9.25 ,,	13 6	9 0
OXFORD		...	...	10.33 ,,	11 0	11 6
DIDCOT		...	...	15 6	15 6	10 0
SOUTHAMPTON (Docks) L. & S.W.		...	9 8 ,,	13 0		6 6
WINCHESTER (Cheesehill)		...	9.40 ,,	8 0		
NEWBURY		...	11.30 ,,			
LAMBOURN		arrive	12.12 p.m.			

The Return Train leaves Lambourn at 6 p.m.

PARTIES of several passengers are requested to kindly communicate with the Station Master at Lambourn on the Saturday before travelling, in order that the necessary accommodation may be provided for the drive.

W. H. H. M. GIPPS, General Manager.

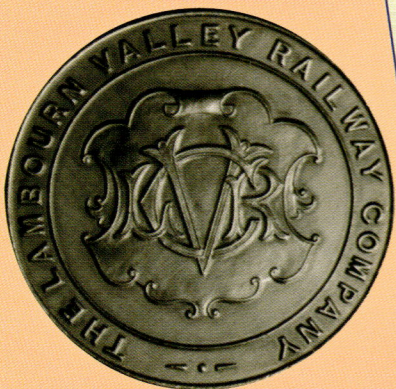

A document dated, 25th February 1904 adds another puzzle to the history of the Lambourn line. On this date Colonel George B Archer-Houblon arranged for "...the acquisition of the Lambourn Valley Capital and Undertaking...", by Sir Alexander Henderson Bart MP, for £50,000. It would appear this was a 'paper transaction', allowing Colonel Archer-Houblon to take what was in effect a back seat from that time on - as well as recoup his investment.

Whether Sir Alexander considered the purchase to be an investment potential is not certain although, of course, the LVR would be sold to the GWR within a year for the same amount - £50.000.

June 5th 1902.

Madam,

Mr Booth of the George Hotel, says he has communicated with you with regard to the provision of the lunch and tea for the weekly Monday excursions to Lambourn during the Summer, and I shall be pleased to know if you are prepared to undertake them for this Season.

What we require, is a nice cold lunch on arrival of the train at 12-3 Cold joints and vegetables, sweets, and cheese, and Afternoon tea consisting of tea, bread and butter, and cake, &c, for those who like it on arrival back from the drive before returning by train, and the price we allow for it is 3/- per head- of course, for those who do no hold through tickets for the tour, you would make your own charges, all liquors, &c being charged extra.

Yours truly,

(signed) W.H.H.M.Gipps.

per

Mrs Penfold,
Red Lion Hotel,
Lambour n.

LAMBOURN VALLEY RAILWAY.

TELEGRAPHIC ADDRESS, "GIPPS, SOUTHAMPTON".

GENERAL MANAGERS OFFICE.

PLEASE REFER

11, Oxford Street.

COPY

Southampton May 6th 1903

Madam,

I enclose a proof bill of the excursions which it is proposed to run to Lambourn this year. Would you pleased let me know if you will be able to arrange for the lunch and Afternoon tea for the passengers at Lambourn on the same terms as previously arranged, viz 3/- per head, to include good cold lunch before drive, and afternoon tea on return (exclusive of liquor).

Yours truly,
(signed) W.H.H.M.Gipps.
per

Mrs Penfold,
Red Lion Hotel,
Lambourn.

The Penfold Family Connection

In an effort to maximise revenue, the independent Lambourn Valley Company ran a series of excursions from at least 1901 onwards to extol the beauties of what was referred to as 'King Alfred's Country' and the Vale of the White Horse.

Connections were provided not just from principal GWR stations, but also from Didcot, Winchester and Southampton, the last three mentioned locations no doubt at the instigation of the General Manager of the LVR Mr Gipps, who simultaneously held the office of Traffic Manager to the Didcot, Newbury & Southampton line, hence the Southampton address for correspondence for the LVR.

Part of the 1901 brochure is reproduced on the opposite page and which also contained historical facts and notes concerning the locations the tour would visit. No doubt to maximise revenue this was not given away free and those interested had to pay 2d. Posters would also have been provided, but a copy of one of these has yet to be located.

The involvement of Mrs Penfold at 'The Red Lion' is apparent for the 1902/3 tours and which from the attached correspondence, would appear to continue a pattern established in earlier years. (See comments on page 11).

It has also been discovered that for these tours, the GWR issued an Edmondson style ticket divided into three different colour sections. The first covered rail travel between Paddington and Newbury, the centre part travel over the Lambourn Valley Railway, and the third the road excursion beyond Lambourn and refreshments prior to the return.

Memorandum.

JOHN PENFOLD,

Red Lion, Lambourn, R.S.O., Berks.

CHARLES 1ST.

Head Quarters Ashdown for 111 Years.

BILLIARDS

Stabling and Loose Boxes Built by Matthew Dawson, Esq.

8 MAY 1903

May 16th 1903

To Gipps Esqr.
D. Sir

We should be very pleased to do the Luncheons etc as you ask. Thanking you in anticipation Remain

Yours truly D Penfold

Former MSWJ 2-4-0 No 1336, leaving Newbury for Lambourn on an unreported date but probably sometime in the late 1930s. The first vehicle is auto-coach No 58, which confirms that this type of vehicle was still in regular service on the line at this time although quite clearly auto-working was not taking place. A second vehicle and a vacuum fitted van make up the service. Throughout the life of the line under the GWR and indeed later under British Railways, services were always described as being of 'one class only'. The only access to the Lambourn line was via the turnout in the left foreground, which would certainly have allowed for a service to run off the branch into the up platform at Newbury, although there was no provision for a passenger service to Lambourn (a down working) to start other than from the bay. The times of certain trains leaving Welford Park were advised to the signalman at Newbury West by telephone, although strictly speaking this was unnecessary, as the act of the Welford Park signalman sending 'Train on line' to Newbury West was in itself an indication that a train was on the way. Just visible also is the nameplate for the signal box. This was ordered from Reading probably around 1908 but certainly coinciding with the rebuilding of the station, it is not believed there was ever a second plate carrying the name affixed to the rear wall. The rebuilding also meant that the small ground-frame, referred to one pages 8/9 was rendered redundant. Accordingly the latter's own cast plate, dating from 1897, NEWBURY LAMBOURN VALLEY GROUND FRAME' was consigned for scrap.

Great Western Trust

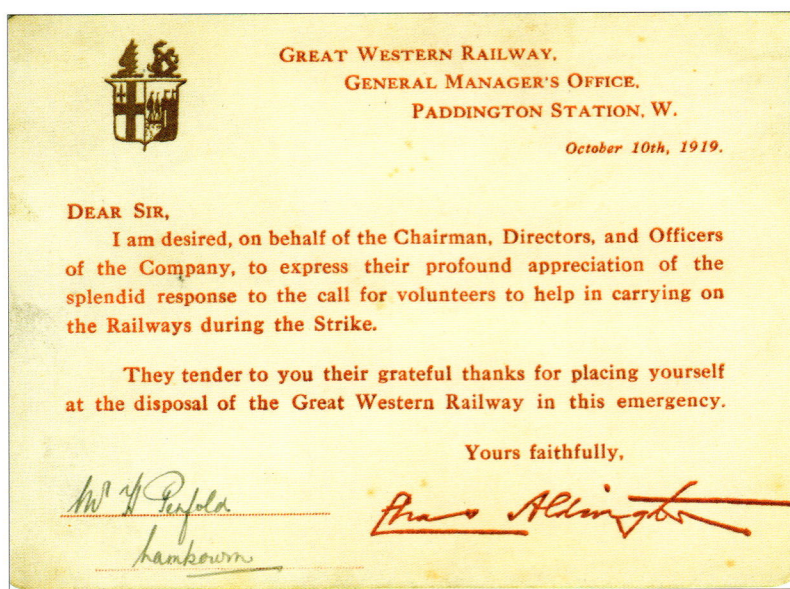

GREAT WESTERN RAILWAY.
GENERAL MANAGER'S OFFICE.
PADDINGTON STATION, W.

October 10th, 1919.

DEAR SIR,

I am desired, on behalf of the Chairman, Directors, and Officers of the Company, to express their profound appreciation of the splendid response to the call for volunteers to help in carrying on the Railways during the Strike.

They tender to you their grateful thanks for placing yourself at the disposal of the Great Western Railway in this emergency.

Yours faithfully,

Card of thanks issued to Mr Harry Penfold, son of John East Penfold, thanking him for his assistance during the 1919 strike. It is signed by the GWR General Manager, Charles Aldington. Mr H Penfold was not a railwayman, he drove a lorry and so whilst he may well have worked on the station during the strike it is perhaps more likely he collected and delivered goods for the GWR in his vehicle.

The Penfold Collection.

WORKING THE LINE

Operation of the Lambourn branch changed little over the years. Indeed, it was only in consequence of the rebuilding at Welford after nationalisation that there could be said to have been any alteration in services and even then affecting only the lower half of the line.

What we do know, of course, are examples of the train services which, again, showed little alteration.

	Lambourn - Newbury	Newbury - Lambourn	Late service Saturday evening	Sunday service
1902	4 *	3 *		
1906	5	5		2
1910	5	5		
1919	5 **	5 **		
1922	5	5		
1923	5	5		
1931	5	5		1
1932	5	5		1
1934	5	5	1	1
1935	5	5	1	1
1936	5	5	1	1
1937	5	5	1	1
1938	5	5	1	1
1939	5	5	1	1
1941	5	5	1	1
1942	5	5	1	1
1944	5	5	1	1

* Two additional up and one additional down trips on Tuesday / Wednesday / opposite Saturday, plus one additional down trip on Monday / Thursday / Saturday.
** Two trips each way operated on Thursday and Saturday only.

What is interesting from the above table is how the service appears to have been curtailed in the immediate post WW1 period. Possibly at this time this was simply due to the restricted availability of both staff and stock in the immediate post-war period.

We know also that, whilst auto working was apparently not used on the line, the May 1914 Carriage Working notices reveal the use of a Trailer and 6-wheel Brake Third that were used for all the branch trips. Additionally an extra car (unspecified) was attached to the 10.45 am Thursday and 12.42 pm Saturday services. Further confirmation that, despite the use of a auto-car, auto-working was not ascribed to, comes from a footnote to the same working notices where it is distinctly noted that; 'Ordinary engines are used on this branch.'

The only logical conclusion as to why auto working was not adopted must be the regular nature of horse box traffic.

Even though the columned figures contain a number of gaps, it is easy to identify the general consensus of services over the years. These figures also relate purely to passenger services, an average of one freight working also taking place each way daily. In additional there would often be one or more horse boxes attached to an ordinary service train, although, if there was a requirement to move more than six horse boxes, a special service was required to be run just for this purpose.

Mixed trains were also known to have been operated at different periods, but this practice had generally ceased on the Lambourn line, as well as elsewhere, by 1930.

Interestingly, it can be seen that, in 1906 at least, there were two services each way on Sundays. Unfortunately, without having access to timetables covering each year we cannot be certain when the Sunday service ceased. I was known to have recommenced, possibly around 1927.

Under the GWR, all trains also ran 'one class only' and there has never been any suggestion of a through service from Lambourn to stations beyond Newbury although through ticketing was of course available.

Notwithstanding the fact that there are obvious gaps in the years quoted opposite, the survival of 'Mark Taking'[1] records assists in filling in some of missing years relative to the services running.

For example, on the 6th March 1920, Welford Park Signal Box was checked and eight trains were recorded. This involved 91 lever movements, the use of the tablet instrument on 16 occasions and nine telephone messages. In addition the signalman used the day to clean the lamps, so bringing his total marks to 433.3, equivalent to a Class 5 grading.

Three years later on Friday 26th October 1923 the number of trains daily had increased to 12 but lamp cleaning was excluded, thus reducing the grade to the lower rate of Class 6. Finally, on 15th February 1946, the number of trains had increased to 14 which, despite the lamps not being taken into consideration, put the grade was once more into Class 5.

The above information is taken from a summary sheet covering the three years in question whilst additional information is available from a copy of the original 1923 record kindly provided by Larry Crosier. This shows that on the date in question the little signal box at Welford Park was open from 7.30 am until 2.00 am the latter time somewhat puzzling, as although it is known there was a regular late goods, this would invariably have been cleared by around 11.00 pm.

The only conclusion is that must have been a number of specials operating on that day, as an hourly audit reveals one train passing between 10.00 pm and 11.00 pm and another between midnight and 1.00 am. Even so the former again raises questions. For the whole of the day, the number of times a lever was pulled or replaced, commensurate with a train passing, varied between 2 and 9. Yet, for the two late trains the figure shot up to no less than 48 for the train before midnight and 18 for the last train of the day. It is perhaps surprising there was no explanatory note attached.

Just as interesting is a footnote to the actual operating of Welford on this occasion, which revealed that two signalman worked the box, one from 7.30 am until 11.00 am and the same man again from 1.00 pm until 5.30 pm. Signalman number two came on duty at 5.30 pm and worked through to the finish. The period from 11.00 am until 1.00 pm was covered by a Signal Porter. The duties of these three men were also detailed. "Book all passengers and collect tickets - makes up cash daily and remits to Lambourn - Form '3928'. Book all parcels and collect cash. Does the work generally of a Station Master except monthly which is done by Lambourn from books and records kept and sent in by signalman. Collects monthly accounts if not remitted by cheque to Lambourn. Cash sent to Lambourn on this date £1 5s 10½d. Cleans, take out and fetch in five signal lamps and indicators. Platform lamps during winter. Supervisory loading of hay and straw sheets and rope - about two trucks daily."

As per the attached signal diagram, it can also be seen that at this time Welford Park still retained access to its single goods siding from the Lambourn end, operation of which was controlled by a ground frame. This was released by the tablet for the Lambourn section. Interestingly, we also have confirmation of what was always believed, in that, "Up Goods Shunting Traffic out comes in on wrong road to get to yard". This latter procedure was confirmed as still being a regular feature of working at Welford Park to the very end, even though there a signal authorising this move was never provided.

(1) 'Marks Taking' might well be described as similar to a Time and Motion study. One or two clerks from Paddington - or wherever - would attend a signal box and record every time the signalman carried out an action. Operating a lever, ringing a bell, the number of times the telephone was used etc. In this way a signal box could be classified at a particular grade, with the men paid according to the grade obtained. Sometimes men would apply for a re-grading on the basis of additional work carried out since the last time the marks were taken.
It was also not unknown for colleagues either side to assist by deliberately sending and then cancelling trains or by making with unnecessary telephone enquiries. That is not to say this occurred everywhere or on every occasion, but such actions would assist in pushing the count upwards, especially if the result would otherwise have been borderline. Of course the man being observed needed the willing assistance of his colleagues and this was not always given.

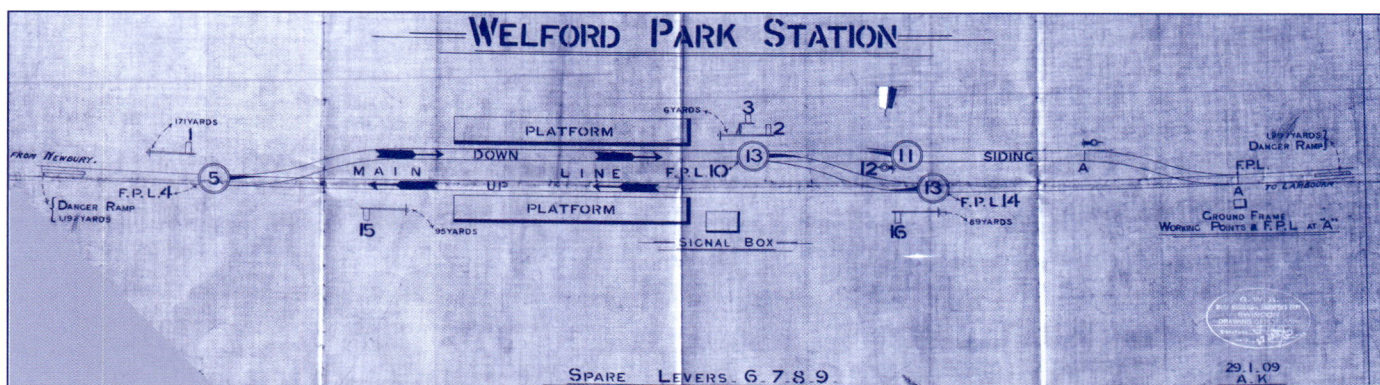

WELFORD PARK STATION

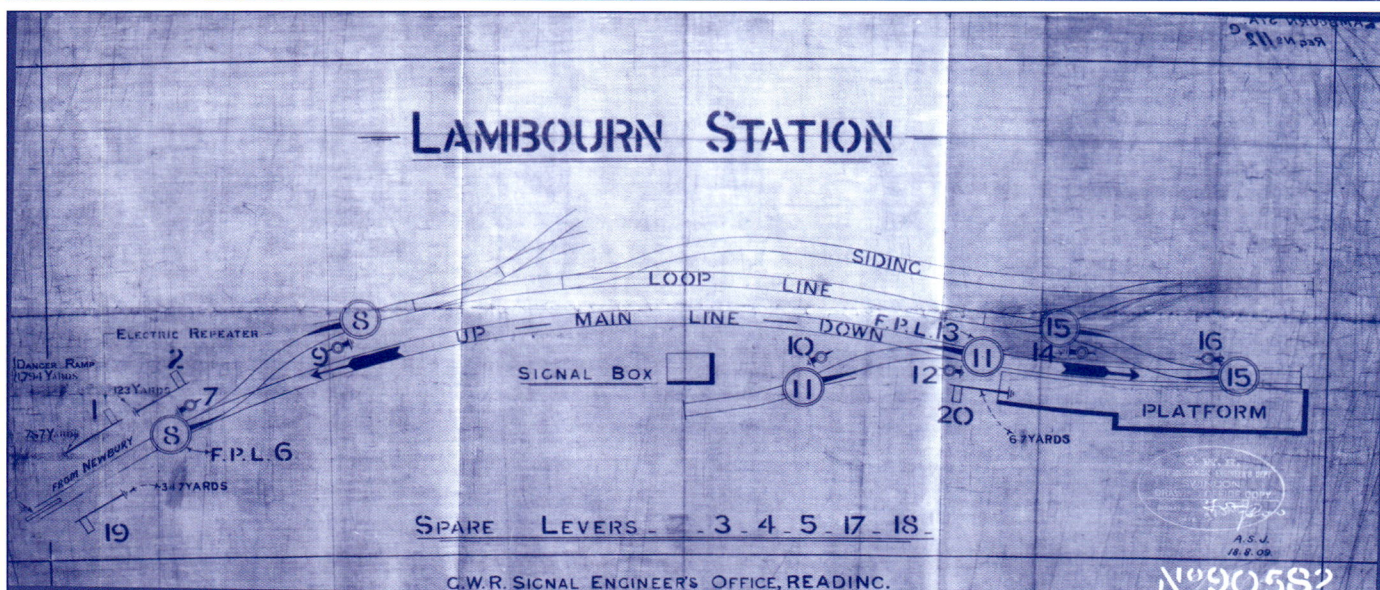

LAMBOURN STATION

This page - Scanned copies of the office linen signal box drawings for Welford Park and Lambourn. The originals are reversed so far as the colours are concerned - white on blue, but this does not reproduce well. Whilst similar diagrams appeared in the original work, that for Welford Park was dated 1953 and after the new frame which followed the provision of the new sidings, had been installed. In the diagram seen here, dating from 17th January 1930, the original layout is shown complete with the ground frame and yard exit at the north end of the site. This GF would have had to have been operated by either the signalman or guard. Notice also that there is no controlling signal allowing direct access into either the goods siding at this point or into the down platform for trains coming from Lambourn. Presumably the official arrangement was for a goods with wagons to pick up, to run right through the station from the Lambourn direction and then set back. Understandably then and considering the light service, the staff adopted a more practical approach and which is referred to in the text. The Lambourn diagram is similarly dated and gives detail of the siding behind the signal box. (The curvature in the track layout is exactly as per the drawing and is not a distortion of the scan.)

In both cases of particular interest is the absence of any distant signals. Instead 'danger ramps' are shown. These were the experimental ATC ramps installed in place of distant signals. A similar installation on the Fairford branch is well known, but, even so, this is possibly the very first time any official drawings making reference to these have been seen. (See page 31 of the original work.)

Why these two drawings were dated at this time is not certain. They certainly depict the layouts at both locations at their peak, as in 1936 the north exit to the yard at Welford and in 1938 the siding behind the signal box at Lambourn were taken out of use. Could it even be that this was the time the ATC ramps were replaced with conventional distant signals?

Left - Lambourn signal box in the early 1950s and of similar design to that at Welford Park. The two structures differed only in so far as the roof style was concerned, one having a pitched roof and the other a hipped design. The good luck horse-show above the door will be noted!

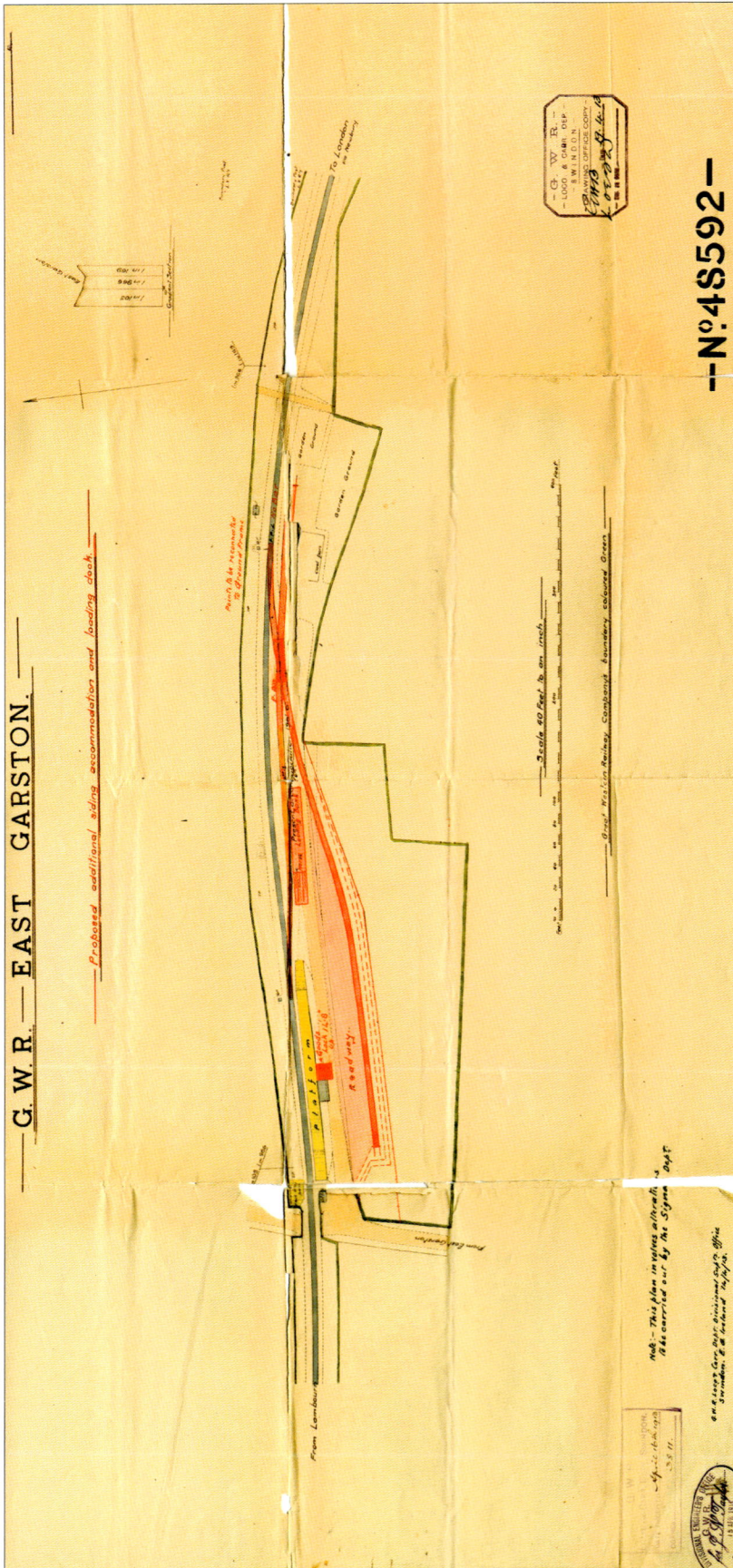

— G.W.R. — EAST GARSTON. —

— N° 48592 —

—— Proposed additional siding accommodation and loading dock

Scale 40 feet to an inch

—— Great Western Railway Company's boundary coloured Green

copy of

Officer	Estimate			Date of signature	Officer's signature
Engineer					
Locomotive Supt.				19.4.13	H. Wright
Signalling Engineer				9.4.1913	A.T. Blackall
Electrical Engineer					
Divisional Supt.				22 March 1913	J. Dunster
District Goods Manager					
Supt. of Line					
Chief Goods Manager					

A 1913 proposal for an extension to the facilities at East Garston. Nothing was known of this suggestion until quite recently and it is certainly not mentioned in the GWR company minute books. Clearly there must have been a considered traffic reason for the extension of facilities, which might normally be ascertained from a study of the 'Traffic Dealt with at Stations' statistics, available for most locations on the GWR. Unfortunately, so far as the Lambourn line is concerned, all the stations on the line were added together to form just one figure and consequently we cannot be certain what event may have caused this exercise to be undertaken. It may have been something as simple as the existing single siding being full for a considerable amount of the year with regular traffic and this additional facility, whilst no doubt useful throughout the year, was considered necessary during harvest time when additional traffic would have been generated. It will also be noted that, had the siding been provided, the layout at East Garston would have been very similar to that provided by the GWR at neighbouring Great Shefford.

To the Directors of
The Great Western Railway Company.

In consideration of your permitting me to walk upon your Line of Railway between 63½ chains and 3 miles 32½ chains on Hambourne valley line and on main line between 54 miles 60 chains and 57 miles and 57 miles 52 chains and 58 miles 69 chains

I do hereby acknowledge and declare that such permission is, and shall at all times be exercised by me, upon the express condition that the Great Western Railway Company are not to be held liable, either to me or to _____ the permission hereby granted; and I do also admit and declare that the Great Western Railway Company are at liberty at any time, and from time to time, either temporarily or wholly, to withdraw such permission.

And I do further undertake and agree that in the event of their at any time or times renewing the same, then and in every such case this Agreement shall be considered as a continuing one and shall extend and apply to any and every such renewal in the same manner and with the like effect as if this Agreement were expressly entered into upon each and every such renewal.

Dated this Sixth day of March One thousand nine hundred and 22

Witness. H. Masters

Above - No 1334 awaiting departure from Newbury. (For more detailed information, see caption on page 31). Trains on the branch, seemingly especially those hauled by these engines, were referred to locally as the 'Lambourn Billie'.

Left - A Walking Permit covering parts of the main Berks & Hants line and also the lower section of the Lambourn branch. (Note the spelling of Lambourn with an 'e' at the end - this was a regular error perpetuated not only by the railway.)

Walking Permits were a common feature of the GWR for many years and were regularly issued to persons who job might involve the need to have regular access to railway premises. The most usual were gamekeepers.

What was obviously being guarded against was any claim for injury against the GWR - the days of being aware of liability are clearly not new!

Even so there was no formal training or certificate in 'track safety' required, whilst the record of injuries to such persons granted a permit was negligible. Common sense was the order of the day.

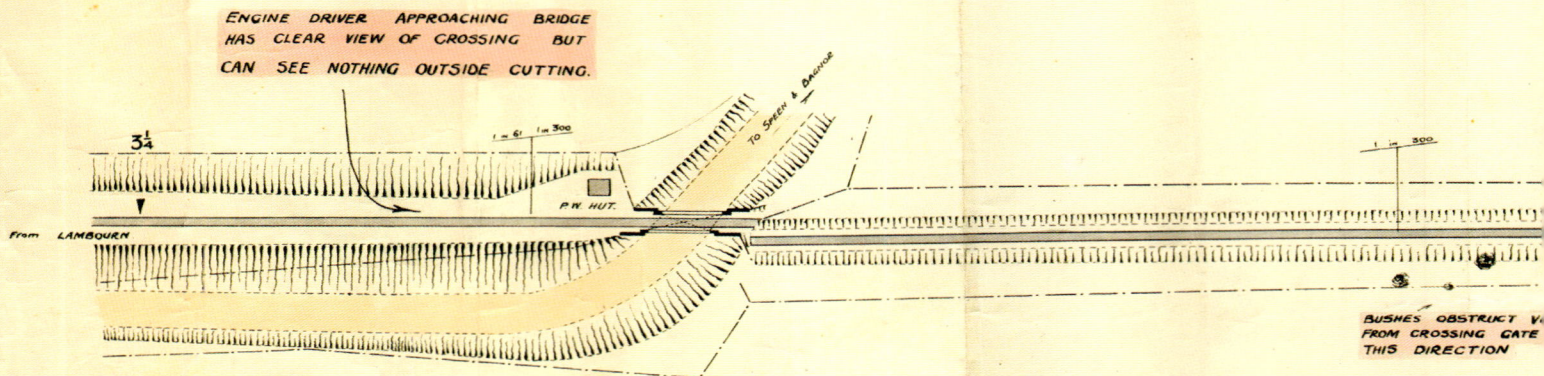

ENGINE DRIVER APPROACHING BRIDGE
HAS CLEAR VIEW OF CROSSING BUT
CAN SEE NOTHING OUTSIDE CUTTING.

A intriguing find rescued from being destroyed from BR archives. (It is included here and whilst slightly out of sequence, benefits form the advantage of coloured reproduction.) The location and plan date are given, 26th January 1942, but after this all becomes conjecture.

What we can realistically assume is that an incident of some sort occurred at Elms Occupation Crossing, although very likely at some time prior to the date of the plan. (The plan will also be noted to have been copied in March 1962 although by this time only the stub to Welford was in occasional use.)

Whether a 'coming together' actually occurred or whether it was a 'close encounter' is uncertain. There is seemingly no record in either Board of Trade accident reports or the local newspaper, although the fact this was wartime could well be the explanation in both cases. We also have no idea as of the time of day of any incident, nor even if it occurred in darkness.

A study of the drawing also suggests that a vehicle, or something similar was approaching the crossing from the west side, at which point there would be little visibility, save for smoke and steam, of a train within a cutting and approaching from the Boxford (Lambourn) direction. The fact that the railway is on a rising gradient of 1-300 towards Stockcross at this point would no doubt mean an engine driver would have 'steam on', but the limited loads and speeds hardly meant there would be much to see outside of the cutting. Likewise any sound would be restricted. Similarly, assuming the incident occurred in autumn / winter, any escaping steam would be more readily visible than during the summer months. (A diesel operated service would be even more difficult to detect and it has to be said that on occasions those using occupation crossings generally did not always ascribe to the 'Stop - Look - Listen' philosophy.

It will be noted also the engine crew would have a view of the crossing itself, but not of the approach paths.

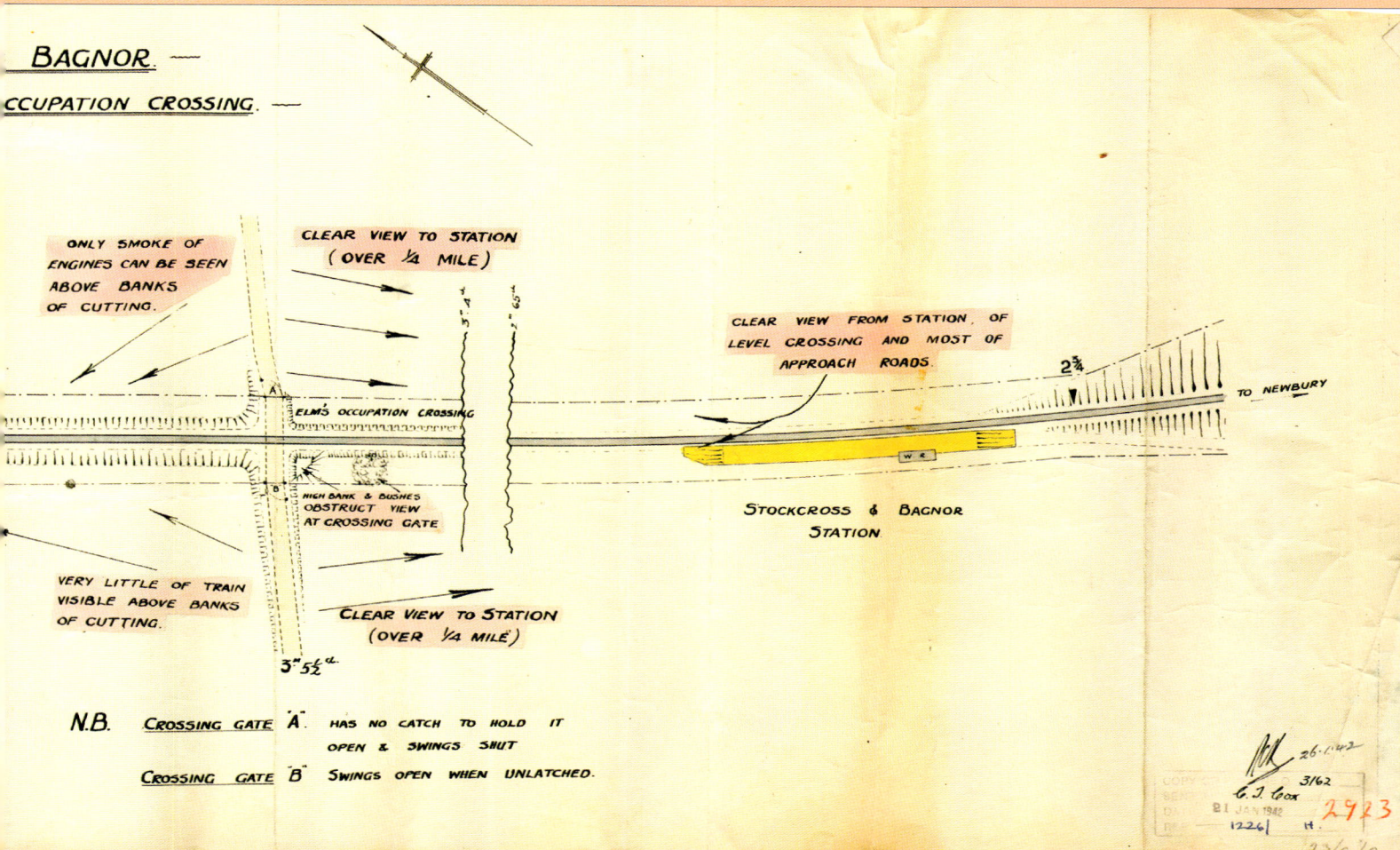

BAGNOR. —

OCCUPATION CROSSING. —

ONLY SMOKE OF ENGINES CAN BE SEEN ABOVE BANKS OF CUTTING.

CLEAR VIEW TO STATION (OVER ¼ MILE)

CLEAR VIEW FROM STATION, OF LEVEL CROSSING AND MOST OF APPROACH ROADS.

TO NEWBURY

ELM'S OCCUPATION CROSSING

HIGH BANK & BUSHES OBSTRUCT VIEW AT CROSSING GATE

STOCKCROSS & BAGNOR STATION

VERY LITTLE OF TRAIN VISIBLE ABOVE BANKS OF CUTTING.

CLEAR VIEW TO STATION (OVER ¼ MILE)

N.B. CROSSING GATE 'A' HAS NO CATCH TO HOLD IT OPEN & SWINGS SHUT

CROSSING GATE 'B' SWINGS OPEN WHEN UNLATCHED.

The plan does not indicate that 'Whistle' boards applicable to approaching trains were provided. Had this been the case then it is likely they would have been shown. Such a provision was usually only provided where a public footpath crossed the line or where the approach to a crossing of any type was subject to limited visibility. Here, in both directions, there was something in the order of 300 yards clear visibility both for the train crew and also for someone on the crossing, which applied in either direction.

It can be assumed that an approaching train would be travelling at no more than 20 mph

Finally, the comments on the crossing gates themselves should be mentioned. Gate 'B' would stay open whereas Gate 'A' needed to be held open - or even wedged. One man having to deal with this as well as drive / lead / herd, whatever, over the crossing would find this difficult and it could well be that something was stationary on the railway whilst Gate 'A' was attended to.

It will be noted also that, for comparison purposes, the view from the station in the opposite direction is also given, whilst at the 20 mph speed stated, an approaching train would have been in view for a maximum of around 30 seconds, if first seen when 300 yards distant.

This was not the only incident to occur on an occupation crossing on the branch, as on an unreported date a van was struck by a train whilst attempting to cross to Maidencourt Farm on the section between Great Shefford and East Garston. The van was carried some considerable distance by the train. (The train driver on the occasion of the Maidencourt accident was Peter Bloomfield.)

LIFE AT LAMBOURN

1930 and 1950

In early 2008 it was a privilege to visit and talk to another former member of staff, Charlie Marshall, who had started work at Lambourn as a Lad Porter in 1948.

Conversation with Charlie revealed detail of the daily life and staff duties at the station, which provide an insight into the railway at this time. This is the first time these memories have been recorded. In addition, perusal of a record of 'marks' carried out at Lambourn in 1930 provides an interesting study.

The marks system has already been described on page 23. Fortunately a similar record has survived relating to Lambourn and although dated for early 1930, actually refer to four separate weeks in 1929. The dates concerned are weeks ending the 16th February, 20th April, 17th August, and 12th October. Over these four weeks it was recorded that respectively 72, 86, 82, and 86 trains ran.

There would be little point in repetition of the comments concerning Welford at this point, although, suffice to say, it was reported that two signalman worked the 'box at Lambourn. Note that the grade is distinctly given here as 'Signalman'. The box was also open from 7.00 am until 11.00 pm "...or after the goods was put away". As such and despite the fact that we do not have access to a working timetable of the period, it would certainly appear that a late goods was a regular feature of the working at this time.

The emphasis on the grade of man employed was made with good reason, as the sheet also contains a lengthy discourse on the additional duties of the signalman, which might then lead to the grade being more accurately described as 'Signal-Porter'.

"Unlock Station Offices (shortly after 7.00 am). Collect tickets off incoming train and shunting 10.20 am to 10.30 am. Fetch and trim four signal lamps. Take out four lamps and attend Parcels Office while staff at dinner. (Then in afternoon) - Collect tickets incoming train and shunting. Attach engine to outgoing train, hook up wagons in yard. Trim two yard and two 'box lamps. Collect tickets (two evening trains.)

Slightly more detail of these tasks is given of these tasks described as; "Extraneous duties performed by Lambourn Signalman. Collect tickets off each morning train daily. Sorting and sending all branch tickets to Audit Office daily. Mondays and Thursday, fetch in, trim and clean, and take out signal lamps. Yard and box lamps daily. Assist in passenger and goods shunting, attach engine to outgoing passenger trains. Go round yard and hook up wagons each evening for 9.00 p.m. goods. Render each Monday to Audit Office coaching stock return. Write out and label all outwards passenger traffic and attend to loading. Assist in taking out, putting in, bales and loading horse box traffic. Look after Parcels Office 7.00 a.m. to 10.00 a.m., 1.00 p.m. to 2.00 p.m., 5.00 p.m. to 6.00 p.m. and 7.50 p.m. to finish. Unlock and lock up morning and night; waiting rooms and offices. Light platform and yard lamps each night as required. Attend to necessary bill posting. Clean and trim roof lamps for horse boxes as required [1] Attend to weight bridge and goods required between 1.00 pm. And 2.00 p.m."

Thus it can be seen that the task of the signalman was far more than dealing with a few trains, although the question must also be asked, was this really the work that the signalman was regularly employed in, or something to again appease the audit?

There could well be two viewpoints. Certainly the role of Signalman at Lambourn would involve periods of inactivity, so it would indeed make sense for other tasks to be assigned. The grade of 'Signal-Porter' was referred to earlier. Conversely, there was a considerable number of other staff employed at Lambourn, Clerks, Porters etc. Therefore it might seem strange then that the 'Signalman' should be required to take on such a multi-functional role. With consideration, possibly the most accurate assessment for the period might well be that the signalman would be expected to assist 'as required' and in whatever role was necessary for the time.

Left - Former MSWJ 2-4-0 No 1334 on Lambourn line services in January 1935. The views here and the one on Page 27 are from a series of five taken by Dr I C Allen on a trip to the Berkshire area in January 1935. (One other, similar view was reproduced in the original book, whilst the fifth shows the engine with a solitary horsebox at Didcot and is consequently out of the scope of the present work. Didcot was also at the time in Berkshire!) Dealing with Page 27 first, this was clearly taken in the Lambourn bay at Newbury with the train waiting to depart. Again the first vehicle would appear to be an auto-trailer - see caption comments page 22. As usual, the locomotive is running 'chimney first' which was certainly more usual although by no means always the case. The lower two views depict the engine on arrival at Lambourn on a subsequent occasion, with the centre photograph showing a horse apparently being loaded. After this the engine will push the train back to enable the release crossover to be cleared after which the engine will again run forward ready to run-around the stock. In this respect it is slightly puzzling that the horse is being loaded at this stage and not after the engine has attached itself to the other end when there would certainly be less noise to disturb the animal. Notice also the locomotive shed is still standing.

Cecil George Rackham - engine driver based at Lambourn and the first of four generations whose male descendents would take the christian name, Cecil.

Cecil began his railway career at Winchester where he is recorded as an Engine Cleaner in 1906/07. His subsequent moves and career are not certain, although it is known he subsequently transferred from Winchester to Lambourn as a driver.

The progression at the time was of course through the grades of Engine Cleaner, then Fireman, until finally reaching Driver, although in both the latter referred to footplate roles, there were 'links' to progress through commencing with shunting, then various goods turns until reaching passenger service. This applied to both Firemen and Drivers.

It was also normal practice for at least two depot moves to take place between Cleaner and Driver, the purpose of which was to gain the maximum experience of different types of work. Consequently we can be certain Cecil would have transferred away from Winchester, before returning again to Winchester this time as a driver. His move to Lambourn came after this and whilst we have no date, assuming he were aged 15-16 as a cleaner, his arrival at Lambourn might well have been around 1930.

At Lambourn there were two sets of driver and firemen, both Cecil and his opposite number, Driver Eggleton, living in Mill Lane.

At Lambourn Cecil was engaged on running trains primarily just to Newbury. It was practice also for most men to have remained within a limited area and so assuming his previous postings had been to perhaps Reading or Didcot, this would have enabled him to maintain some route knowledge of the area around Newbury.

The Lambourn posting was also in itself somewhat specialist. With only two crews present, these would have to be men who could be trusted to work with the minimal supervision.

As such it might sound an idyllic posting, but all good things come to an end and that end occurred in 1937 when the diesel railcar serving commenced consequent upon which the engine shed closed. It was still standing, although unused, a year later. (Possibly the GWR deliberately retained the facilities in the event of the diesel railcars not being deemed suitable for use on a permanent basis.) The railcars were now based at Reading and whilst the daily goods remained steam hauled, the engine for this was no longer stabled at Lambourn.

Cecil and his family, there were seven children, thus moved to Didcot and where he continued his career from that depot. During the war years he was known to have been employed shunting the army depot at nearby Milton and which might seem a retrograde step for a man who had previously been on passenger work. Whether this was his sole task or whether there were particular reasons for this work, we cannot be certain.

He remained at Didcot until retirement, after which he returned to Lambourn where his descendents still live.

The photograph shows Cecil alongside one of the former MSWJ 2-4-0s at the Lambourn buffer stops, complete with engine oil can but without the pipe he often smoked. It is most likely the view was taken during his period at Lambourn although Didcot men would also work one Sunday train across the branch using an engine of this type.

His grandson also recalls that as a boy he was taken by an Aunt to the station to deliver Cecil's dinner around 3.00 pm.

Cecil Rackham Collection.

LIFE AT LAMBOURN 1930 and 1950

A more accurate record of life at the station, this time around 1948, can be gleaned first hand from former Charlie Marshall who was interviewed for the post by the Station Master; Stan Knapp. Stan was remembered as a very laid back character although even so at times he did loose his temper.

Charlie would work on either early or late turn, the former starting at 6.55 am. Assuming he was on the early shift, access to the site would be via the side gate and the first task would be to visit the signal box - already opened - and collect the keys to the main gate and offices.

The offices to be unlocked were those of the Station Master and the booking office, both of which would also have to have their respective grates cleared and fires laid and lit - dependent of course upon the time of year. At the same time the same offices were dusted.

Immediately after this, Charlie would walk along the line to Bockhampton Crossing, 10 minutes being allowed for the purpose. At Bockhampton the gates would be opened ready for the departure of the 8.00 am diesel to Newbury, this service sometimes having a van attached at the rear. As the diesel passed it was time to phone Tom Liddiard at East Garston to advise him of the departure. Tom would thus be aware of the actual running time of the service and could expect the train seven to eight minutes later.

The gates were then closed across the railway again and a further 10 minute walk would ensue; back to the station where there was sometimes a cup of tea ready for him.

The next task was again housekeeping, the platform swept if necessary and the ladies and gentleman's toilets cleaned. The mops for this purpose were kept near the fire buckets whilst disinfectant was housed in the metal pagoda store on the platform.

During the period in question it was customary for two spare coaches to be stabled at Lambourn and these needed to be swept out daily. Additionally, once a week, the carriage windows were cleaned with brick dust whilst a hose was used to refill the roof water tanks.

Cleaning the coaches though could not be accomplished in one go, as part way through it was necessary to break off and walk down to Bockhampton ready to have the gates open for the arrival of the 9.25 am passenger service from Newbury, due at Lambourn at 10.01 am. Charlie would now have the opportunity for a short break at the crossing, as he was required to remain here until the same working returned to Newbury having left Lambourn at 10.40 am.

Upon his own return to Lambourn, he continued with jobs as required, taking his lunch at 11.15 am although by the time he reached home he was left with only about 10 minutes indoors.

In addition to cleaning and crossing duties, he was expected to book parcels arriving for onward despatch. The railway lorry would have arrived earlier and also left. This meant that if any perishables came by train during the morning, Charlie was expected to deliver these himself.

Occasionally there were also horseboxes to clean out. These might have arrived as part of a special working late the previous night, the horses being walked from the station to their respective stable yards whilst Charlie's task was to clean out the horse boxes.

Late turn duty commenced at 12.45 pm, with the need to attend to every arrival and departure at Bockhampton, except on Saturday evening when the crew of the final service from Newbury and its corresponding return empty saw to the gates themselves.

(1) A number of roof lamps for horseboxes were allocated specifically to Lambourn and labelled as such - presumably with a metal plate. At least one occasion is known when these were not returned as required and a 'lost' memorandum was sent.

Lambourn Lad Porters; left - Charlie Marshall and right - Alan Marshall (no relation), who lived at Welford and who took over from Charlie after the latter's move to be signalman at Welford. They are depicted outside the pagoda store; the parcels office is just visible on the right.
This page and page 35, Charlie Marshall Collection

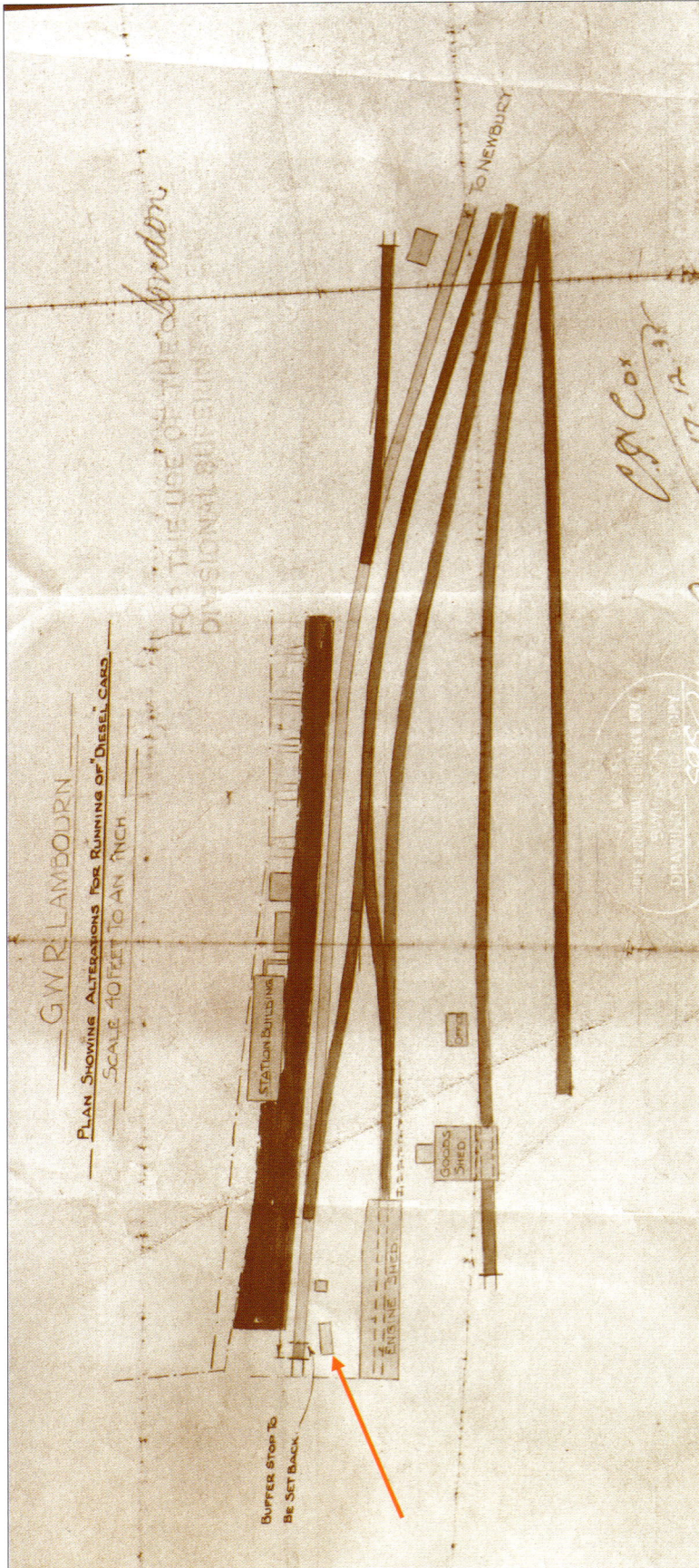

Necessary alterations at Lambourn consequent upon the introduction of the railcars. The plan shows how the distance between the toe of the turnout (see Nos 15 and 16 on the signalling plan on page 25) and the buffer stop, had to be increased in order to accommodate a run round for the railcar when necessary. The plan was dated December 1935, well over a year in advance of when the diesel service actually commenced. A similar alteration was effected to the Lambourn bay at Newbury and for the same reason. (The arrow indicates what was the pump house).

It is difficult to notice this extension from photographs, but an extension it certainly was, albeit it could hardly be said to be the start of the once suggested expansion of the route beyond Lambourn!

Bernard Smith recalls that whilst the diesel railcars were certainly modern for the time, there were aspects of the design that were decidedly primitive and appeared not to have been completely thought through. One of these was the heater for the passenger compartment and which involved a separate exhaust mid way along the roof line.

This heater had a tendency to smoke when in operation, whilst it was likewise not unknown to progress to one stage further and actually catch fire, threatening to set the complete vehicle alight. As such all staff were vigilant should volumes of smoke start issuing. Such was the case at Newbury one day when Car No. 19 was waiting in the Lambourn bay. Bernard was working as a Lad in the Parcels Office, the building which was located on the platform directly at the end of the Lambourn bay. (This was prior to his time as a signalman at Welford, as is described later.) Upon emerging from the office, the staff were treated to the sight of the Newbury Station Master, Mr John Miller, on all fours on top of the roof of the car, judiciously pouring sand into the exhaust of the heater. Whether by luck or through the actions of Mr Miller, the incident did not develop further.

"...Tails from the Riverbank..."

(with due acknowledgement to Johnny Morris of course!)

Charlie Marshall freely admits that there were occasional perks to his task of attending to the crossing gates at Bockhampton. One of these was the opportunity to fish in the nearby River Lambourn. For this purpose he would deliberately go to work early and set a line in the river behind the railway hut seen in the distance. The chance to catch a fish was only possible about once a month, but even so it was a welcome. (The results can be seen in the photograph on page 60.) The view is looking from the Lambourn direction towards the crossing.
Following his time at Lambourn, Charlie became a signalman at Welford Park - see page 66.

The Diesel Railcars

The introduction of Diesel Railcar No 18 has been documented previously. What is new however, is this wonderful contemporary record which first appeared in *THE HISTORY OF THE GREAT WESTERN DIESEL RAILCARS* by Colin Judge - published Oxford Publishing Company 1986 and republished by Noodle Books in 2008. It was entitled "False Alarm - or two horns with a single note".

"There's a bit of an argument on at Lambourn, where AEC diesel railcar No 18 is working the branch line traffic. And it's all because one evening, recently, the railcar's driver's sleeve accidentally touched the electric horn button.

"The amazing result of this was that the Lambourn Fire Brigade - or at least most of it - turned out with its engine and full fire fighting paraphernalia.

"Where's the fire? Demanded the men of the brigade, on arrival at the Police Station.

"Fire, queried the Sergeant, I've never sounded the alarm for the fire.

"So in due course the Captain went along to the Station Master of Lambourn (GWR) then the argument started.

"You can't do that sort of thing, said the Captain. Why the next time your driver presses his horn button accidentally the Brigade will turn out again.

"It's a bit difficult I admit, replied the Station Master, because one day there might be a real fire, and your men might think the alarm was only that.........railcar again, and take no notice at all.

"I had my horn first, said the Captain.

"Well I don't see how the railcar horn can be altered, said the Station Master. There's been a lot of experimenting before that particular note was decided upon.

"Something's got to be done about it, added the Captain, very heatedly.

"Well what can I do?, asked the Station Master. And so the argument continues. Meanwhile Lambourn laughs and laughs and laughs."

A further record from the same source referred to the driver of the Lambourn railcar reporting that on 22nd June 1939 the sand injectors had failed to operate in wet conditions. An investigation was carried out immediately, including alterations to the outlet pipes in an attempt to promote a better flow of sand. A test was carried out on the branch on the 4th July which commenced with the sanders working correctly at Newbury. Upon arrival at Lambourn though, the left hand sander failed to operate, necessitating prolonged braking and the vehicle sliding towards the buffer stops. It was concluded the sand might be too fine, whilst, in addition, the sandboxes were thoroughly cleaned out. They were found to contain waste paper, other debris plus a dead mouse. Subsequent operation was satisfactory.

Above - Carriers guarantee for Albert Bracey. Mr Bracey was one of several local carriers engaged by the GWR to deliver and collect parcels on their behalf at rural stations, such as Lambourn. The Bracey family were synonymous with Lambourn for many years whilst a descendent would also achieve high office on British Railways in later years. Notice too the name of one of the guarantors - Arthur Knapp, presumably a forbearer of Stan Knapp, destined to become the last Station Master at Lambourn. The cartage agreement between the GWR and Mr Bracey continued until 31st December 1947 at which point it was terminated by the GWR in consequence of the introduction of a railway vehicle under what was termed the 'zonal' scheme.

Opposite page - 57xx No 4606, waiting in the Lambourn bay at Newbury with the last service of the day down the branch, Saturday 15th May 1959. Four down and three up services were all that was left in the timetable to serve the line in its final year of operation. Departure was scheduled for 5.20 pm, after which the train would call at each of the stopping places in turn before arrival at Lambourn for 6.00 pm. The engine would then have just five minutes to run round before returning to Newbury - once more all stations. After that the line would effectively go to sleep until Monday morning.

To LAMBOURN
- in Colour

4606

ONE DOG [ACCOMPANYING PASSENGER]

Welford Park to

ANY STATION NOT EXCEEDING
3 MILES DISTANT

(W)   For conditions see over   Rate 0 93

Welford Park, 5.41 pm, 16th May 1959.

4606 has arrived with the 5.20 pm from Newbury, scheduled to be a Diesel turn but obviously not so on this occasion. The train is crossing No 2221 running light engine back to Newbury, although again unusual as this should really be empty coaching stock from the 4.15 pm Newbury to Lambourn. On weekdays the latter service was used by returning school children.

East Garston.

Following the withdrawal of the remaining 'Dean Goods' and MSWJ 2-4-0s in the early 1950s, the Western Region had little option but to approve the use of more modern and therefore heavier steam engines on the branch. This then led to 57xx tank engines and 22xx tender engines appearing on services, a situation that was to last for the remaining life of the line.

East Garston

The classic view of a rural railway. A single coach - ironically also to a former LMS design is taken north in the summer of 1959 by, we are told, 87xx series 0-6-0PT No 9749, in the final full year of operation. Three crew would have been on the train, Driver, Fireman, and Guard. Add to them the station staff at Welford, Shefford, East Garston, and Lambourn, plus of course the hidden but equally important permanent-way staff and it starts to become apparent why closure took place. Economics can never compensate for the loss of a scene such as this. The quintessentially British rural railway, at its very best.

G H Hunt / Colour Rail BRW1560

Colour views of the other intermediate stations appear conspicuous by their absence. The discovery, then, of these views of Speen and Eastbury were a welcome addition. Regretfully, details of the photographer are not recorded - did he take others? That at Speen could well be a munitions train for Welford, although it is difficult to determine if it was recorded pre or post closure to passenger traffic. Notice also the staff 'privvy' which is not seen in any other views of the station. At Eastbury we see a pannier tank on its way back to Newbury with just two potential passengers waiting. The chocolate and cream 1950s Western Region colour scheme, which replaced GWR light and dark stone, is also prevalent.

Unfortunately it has not been possible to locate any original Lambourn Valley Railway tickets to illustrate this work. We know a number survive, as black and white photocopies were kindly provided to us. In style they were similar to later GWR / BR tickets. It is believed several were on display at the 1998 centenary exhibition held at Lambourn.

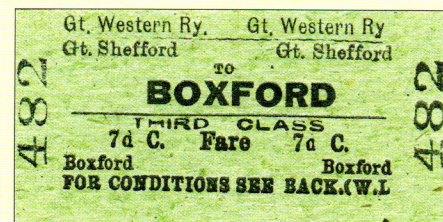

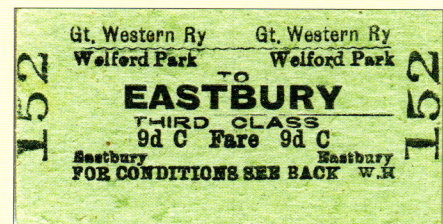

Upper - Lambourn 1950. The diesel railcar is seen in the run-round loop, so may either be in the process of running round a hidden vehicle or possibly coming back to collect one from the yard. In the background coal is being unloaded, whilst a former slip-coach is stabled on the site of the former engine shed, ready to strengthen a service when necessary.

J H Moss / Colour Rail GW53.

Lower - Storm clouds over Lambourn. There is evidence of fresh ballasting to the run round loop. One would hope such work was not undertaken as a means of manipulating costs.

Inset - *Celebration time at Lambourn 1928, following the return home of the Derby winner 'Felstead'. The horse was returned to his home area by special train - hauled by a open cab 'Pannier Tank'. Such was the celebration at Lambourn that crowds thronged the station including an impromptu jazz bank which led the procession through the town, where a number of flags were flown and back to the stables.*

The Penfold Collection

This and previous page - Steam power on the branch in the early BR era. Former MSWJ No 1335 and 'Dean Goods' No 2573 are seen. No 1335 is seen heading south from East Garston with the Old Vicarage, now Trinity Cottage, visible in the background. The location of the view of No 2573 is not recorded. The restricted axle loading on the branch was one of the reasons for the retention of the three MSWJ engines of this type, way beyond what would normally have been their expected life. Together with the slightly larger 0-6-0 'Dean Goods' design, these were the only tender engines then permitted to work the line. Tank engines were similarly restricted, meaning a pair of '850' class saddle tanks Nos 1925 and 2007 were retained at Reading shed solely for the Lambourn line services. These three types of steam locomotive plus the diesel railcars thus made for the complete fleet of motive power that could work on the line until the early 1950s. After this date and as discussed in the final chapter, the chief civil engineer authorised the use of heavier engines, partly due to the pending withdrawal of the three steam types mentioned and also because of the likely requirements of the anticipated military line being built from Welford Park. Indeed, as referred to in the final chapter, the potential lack of suitable steam motive power for the branch, from the early 1950s onwards, may well have been one of the reasons Paddington were keen to close the route and thus avoid expenditure on necessary strengthening - what this remedial strengthening work would have been has not been established. The military line from Welford may well be referred to as the having afforded the branch a respite of several years. In both views seen, traffic may have been limited, but that was still no excuse for not maintaining standards. The permanent way gangs neat furrowing of the cess and tidy ballast were still typical of the railway in the immediate years following nationalisation.

J F Russell Smith / National Railway Museum

Variations in steam motive power on Lambourn services. Top is former MSWJ 2-4-0 No 1336, having left Newbury and running parallel with the main line westwards, just at the point where the branch begins to diverge from the main line. The houses in the background front St Michaels Road, 12th March 1948. Lower - former Cambrian Railway 0-6-0 No 908 at the terminus on 26th March 1937. In the background and against the loading dock stand a number of horse boxes, evidence of a special working either having arrived or being made ready to depart. A number of private owner coal wagons can also be seen including those lettered' Wilmer' and 'Ricketts'. Both were probably coal suppliers' vehicles, as it is not believed any of the merchants on the branch ever possessed there own rail vehicles. *Great Western Trust and Roger Carpenter*

A COMMUNITY RAILWAY

S hoppers used it, schoolchildren used it, the racehorse fraternity used it, households used it, all taking for granted that much of what was on sale in the village shops throughout the valley, including of course at Lambourn, came by rail. And then it warmed their houses, coal being regularly transported in wagons to Lambourn as well as on a semi-regular basis to Welford, Shefford, and East Garston. Of course the farmers and the military used it. The Lambourn line was the epitome of a community railway at a time when the populace were content with a quieter life than is commonplace today. Indeed' this was a community whose weekly highlight might well be a trip into Newbury for a visit to the cinema or to a dance at the Corn Exchange. After that it was a return to the countryside and an insular lifestyle once more. A lifestyle as alien to us now as a modern 21st century one would have seemed to an earlier generation.

Lambourn bound from Great Shefford. The diesel railcars were a common sight on the branch from 1937 through to the end, with commensurate saving of one man in operation. Both Driver and Guard can be seen here in what is probably early BR days. The vehicle is one of the later batch of cars built at Swindon from 1938 onwards, on chassis assembled by AEC at Southall.
Maurice Earley

Above - 22xx No 3210 leaving East Garston for Eastbury with the 4.12 pm Newbury to Lambourn service, 5th September 1959. Judging from the numbers of droplights in the down position this was obviously a warm day. This particular afternoon service regularly consisted of two coaches, as it was used by older schoolchildren returning from Newbury.

Ian Allan Library

Opposite upper - The older variant of 0-6-0 used on the line. 'Dean Goods' No 2552, departing from Welford northwards, sometime prior to 1953. The lack of obvious patronage will be noted. This particular engine remained in service until May 1954. In later years and during the time the military connection was in use, there was additional traffic from Welford in the form of service personnel from the Air Base. It was also not unknown for a group of men to appear just before the train was due, clutching travel warrants and needing to exchange these for rail tickets. Takings would increase dramatically on these occasions. Similarly, it was not unknown for the first empty stock working on the line and likewise the last return, if running empty, to carry service personnel if required. At Welford 'Local instructions' permitted for 'Shunting outside of the Up Home Signal' if required, although the rules would only permit this when a train had not been accepted from Lambourn. On one occasion this condition was not strictly applied and although no collision resulted there were a few embarrassed faces.

Maurice Earley

Opposite lower - A Pannier Tank taking water prior to running round it's single coach train at Lambourn. Harold Gasson, in his 'Firing Days' series of books, refers to working the Sunday service when a young fireman at Didcot. According to Harold it was necessary to pump water at Lambourn on occasions, for which purpose the whistle on the locomotive was removed and a pipe, attached to a donkey engine, substituted. This, though, would use copious amounts of steam to operate, meaning that any gain in water level within the tank was offset by having to replenish the engine supply before they could depart.

Great Western Trust

Above - Hard to imagine today, but the principal commodity transported by rail was coal, whilst local produce would also be sent out. Here former MSWJ 2-4-0 No 1335 is depicted northbound (well, north west really), near to Boxford sometime in 1951 with five wagons in tow, the first at least destined for one of the merchants. It is not possible to determine if the remaining vehicles were similarly loaded, although, if not, they had no doubt been 'ordered' via the telegraph system for use in carrying goods away. This particular loco was one of the three similar engines still surviving at that time, although it would be withdrawn the following year. The class were renowned for struggling up the gradient to Speen and would try and take a run as far as Speen crossing, all the way from Newbury.　　　　　　　　　　　　　　　*P Ransom Wallis*

Above - Taken sometime during 1940, this is a view of a Lambourn goods train, believed to be returning to Newbury, the exact location is not recorded. As locomotives generally seemed to work chimney first towards Lambourn, hence the assumption above. Throughout the majority of the life of the line there was just one specific goods train each way daily, although, additionally, certain services could also run as 'mixed' when required. This meant the inclusion of a horse box or other braked vehicle. The signs on the gates of the occupation crossing will be noted and are typical, not just of the Lambourn line, but of numerous other routes where a warning to 'Shut The Gate' and 'Not to Trespass' were provided.

S Pearce Higgins / National Railway Museum

Opposite lower - The same engine as in the view opposite top, seen at Welford Park, again during 1951 and probably on the same date. In his hand the driver / fireman has the token carrier and token, although whether he is about to give this up, having brought it through from Newbury, or if it is has just been received it for the continuation of the journey to Lambourn is not clear. I think the former is more likely, especially as it appears the Guard is walking forward rather than returning to his van. The time would be sometime between 12.50 pm and 1.05 pm, during which period the service would wait to cross with the 12.40 pm passenger service from Lambourn, due at Welford Park at 1.00 pm. The freight took a leisurely one hour 40 minutes for its 12½ mile journey from Newbury, stopping to drop off and collect any vehicles as required at Boxford, Great Shefford, and East Garston. Five minutes were also allowed for opening and closing the crossing gates at Speen. Of course, should there be no traffic for the intermediate stations then the arrival time at Lambourn might well be earlier. (The signalman at Lambourn would be advised of this and so be aware of approximately when the service was likely to arrive.) After shunting the yard at Lambourn, the returning freight had to wait for the arrival, at 2.40 pm, of the 2.00 pm passenger from Newbury. Departure of the goods was scheduled for 2.47 pm, calling as required at Great Shefford and Welford Park. At the latter location any wagons would be dealt with, as access to the solitary goods siding had, for some years only been available to trains heading in the Newbury direction. To be fair, general goods traffic to and from Welford Park was very limited. Newbury would be reached at 3.30 pm.

P Ransom Wallis

Meanwhile, at Lambourn itself the yard appears very quiet on Saturday 8th May 1954. Standing in the siding to the left are a number of vehicles including it will be noted a container. To the right is a horsebox branded 'Return to Lambourn', and also a gas tank vehicle - 'Cordon'. This would normally be stabled at the end of the siding and was used to replenish the tanks on vehicles, by this stage usually just horse boxes, that were illuminated in this way. Years ago it was rumoured that the straw within the empty horse boxes was used as a soft place to lie and where a particularly well endowed guard would entertain certain of the female population from the town. Notice the engine, just visible to the right.

Norman Simmons / Hugh Davis

FATALITY

On a unreported date a fatality occurred at Lambourn when a Gardener, Robert Maisey, was run over by the engine of the last train from Newbury. It was thought Mr Maisey had been taking a short cut across the line with the simple intention of buying an evening paper. At this point he was struck by the engine in the course of running round its coaches.

Upper - Along the line, at Speen. Edith McCartney watches as the engine and single coach leave Speen destined for West Fields and Newbury. The lack of patronage will be noted whilst just visible on the end of the ticket office wall is the dreaded notice advising of closure.

Lower - Snapshot at East Garston, as a 'Dean Goods' 0-6-0 awaits departure for Eastbury and Lambourn. The obligatory lamp on the tender is missing although no doubt the more important tail lamp was present. The train, it will be no noted, also consists of two coaches both seemingly of 'Toplight' design.

Norman Simmons / Hugh Davis

Opposite lower - An unidentified, later series Pannier Tank against the buffers at Lambourn on a wet 10th October 1959. The 'Cordon' will also be seen in its more usual position. Had the plans of much earlier came to fruition, instead of a dead end here the route might have continued towards Wantage, or possibly, as has been rumoured, to Shrivenham or Swindon. The crew are taking advantage of the engine cab to shelter from the rain, whilst also waiting for the point to be changed allowing them to run-round. Motor access to the goods yard was via the metalled road passing on the far side of the white painted barrier. The fireman has already placed the single lamp in place on the bunker ready for the return journey.

Martin Galley

Welford Park around 7.13 am on a weekday morning. The diesel railcar is arriving at the station with the 6.50 News and Parcels service, due at Lambourn at 7.35 am. This in turn would form the first Up train of the day, leaving Lambourn at 8.00 am and if necessary drawing one or more horseboxes. In theory, and assuming no breakdowns occurred, the vehicle would spend the rest of the day shuttling between Newbury and Lambourn making its last trip empty back from Lambourn at 8.15 pm. It would then return to its home depot at Reading for servicing. In this way, with one exception, all the passenger services on the branch were worked by the diesel unit. The exception was the 4.15 pm service from Newbury which remained steam operated. One additional return journey was made on a Saturday evening allowing an evening out in Newbury. Token exchanges with the driver of the diesel were made using a special small stick, into which the single line token would be placed, this was in place of the conventional large carrier used for steam engines.

Horse boxes, or, as the railway deemed them, 'tail traffic', were invariably a feature of the morning services. Similarly, to allow time to reach the destination, any horse box special would also be a morning working. Indeed, Bernard can only recall one occasion when an outgoing horse box special ran during the afternoon, at around 2.00 pm. (It is a matter of some regret that despite the obvious importance of horse box traffic to the line and views of the occasional horse box attached to the rear of a passenger service, no views of complete trains of this type on the line itself have been discovered.)

The photograph was taken by Bernard Smith, who had arrived at 6.50 am for an early turn duty at Welford Park signal box. This shift would last until 2.00 pm. He recounts that the diesel units could always be heard approaching from some way off, as the sound was so different. This was especially so on a cold morning with still air, when the sound would carry even as it left Lambourn six miles distant. Normally the drivers operated with just one engine running, keeping, it seemed, the second 'in reserve'. This was a shrewd move, as on a number of occasions one of the engines (possibly its transmission) would fail leaving broken bits littering the track. These the driver would collect and place in a bucket that was carried on board, the second engine then being started up but belching a cloud of black smoke in the process. After that the remainder of the duty would be completed, although the ability to haul any 'tail traffic' was seriously impaired.

Photo - Bernard Smith

LIFE AT WELFORD PARK
The memories of Bernard 'Curly' Smith

S taff memories are a vital and integral part of any attempt at recalling the history of a railway line. The facts, dates and figures survive, but without the personal account of how everything comes together, any attempt at recalling every day working would be a cold analysis of surmise and conjecture. Bernard Smith changed all that, he, along with several former colleagues, have, over the years willingly given of their time and memories and been all too happy to pass on to successive generations recollections of their own working lives. Sometimes these men - and women - spent all of their time in a single task. With others it was for lesser periods. The timescale, though, is not important It is the willingness to share which is more so. Bernard, thank you. The fact you also took some damned good photographs helps as well!

Another of Bernard's photographs although this time the railcar has departed north and all will be quiet for at least an hour, save the receipt of 'Train out of Section' from Lambourn to be followed in quick succession by another request 5-1-3 on the bell, meaning 'Is Line Clear for Diesel Railcar?' and ready for the return working. In the background a single wagon can be seen in the goods siding, although more often this would be empty for long periods. Further left against the trees is a permanent way hut, the home base for the gang who looked after the section between Boxford and Great Shefford. In Bernard's time at Welford, the Ganger for this stretch was Bob Hopkins.

Snapshots from Bernard Smith during his time as signalman at Welford Park.

Bernard had started at Newbury as a Lad Porter in the Parcels Department during 1946. He recalls being interviewed for the job by Mr Lowe - '"...Pill-Box Hat and Prinz-Nez Glasses..."'. A few years later he was advised of a signalling vacancy learning his first signal box at Litchfield on the Winchester route south from Newbury

Shortly afterwards he was told of a signalman's vacancy at Welford Park, and upon the suggestion of the District Inspector at Newbury, Bob Sullivan, applied for and was successful in obtaining the post. Bernard spend nine years at Welford Park from 1950 until leaving the railway in early 1959. (Interspersed with one year off when he broke his leg in a motor-cycle accident. The railway though kept his position open.) He still looks back on his time at Welford Park as being one of the happiest times of his working life.

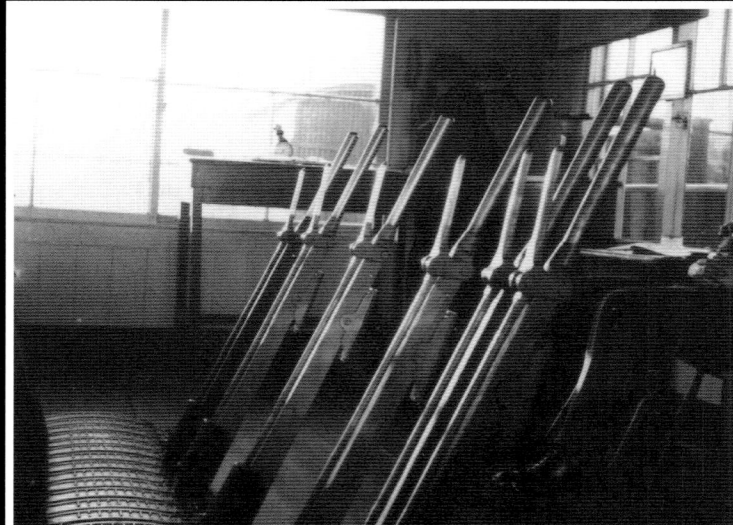

LIFE AT WELFORD PARK

Bernard Smith's memories of his time at Welford Park cover not only his life as a signalman. He was not just signalman but was responsible for the issue of tickets as well. Because the railway was very much a separate entity from the rest of the system, he can recount stories from elsewhere on the branch.

At Speen, for example, where the Porter in Charge for some time on the morning shift was Edith McCartney. Speen also had no direct water supply, so instead staff would obtain supplies by can from Mrs Osborne. Mrs Osborne also kept geese. Invariably they would forage on the track near the station and were regularly fed by the train crews. Possibly this was in a vain attempt to one day bag a specimen, although in the event the birds were too wily and

Below - Snapshots at Speen. Bernard was a motor-cycle enthusiast and consequently friendly with several others of like mind. One of his friends, Johnny 'Mitch' Mitchell, is seen here with his machine on the platform at Speen. 'Mitch' also had the dubious distinction of one day skidding his machine into the gates at Speen crossing. In 1955 Roy Flitter arrived to take on the Porter's job at Speen with relief for him arranged when required by Mr Miller, the then Newbury Station Master. Roy recalls riding pillion on the rear of Stan Taylor's motorcycles - one of Bernard's friends, whilst carrying a bucket of whitewash on one side and a brush on the other side. This was as far as the next station along the branch at Stockcross & Bagnor, where Roy had the task of painting the white line along the platform edge. Roy's turn of duty started at 7.30 am, after the first empty train had passed. The driver and guard of the empty working responsible for opening and closing the gates at the level crossing themselves, otherwise it was the job of the porter at Speen to do this each time. The same arrangement applied for the last train back to Newbury in the evening where driver and guard were again responsible. The ticket office at Speen was locked with a large key hung on a nail and 'hidden' by the side of the actual door. Despite this limited security no instance was recalled of the place ever having been unlawfully entered.

Opposite top left - Welford Park signal box, mid way between Newbury and Lambourn. The provision of the passing loop and signal box here made Welford the most important operational point between the two ends of the line, although its traffic receipts were amongst the least. To the right the small waiting shelter survives in preservation at Didcot. In practice it was rarely used for its intended purpose, most passengers waiting in the warmth of the signal box.

Opposite top right - Charlie Marshall at Welford with a fish 'acquired' from the nearby River Lambourn. (Bernard has another photograph of the same fish laid against a ruler to indicate its size.)

Bottom left - the original, left, and replacement, right, lever frames inside the signal box. The new frame was installed in September 1953 and had 23 levers instead of the previous 16. This was because of the provision of new sidings for the connection to RAF Welford - see page 71. Bernard recalled that the old levers and brass plates were just thrown into a wagon outside. "I could have had what I wanted but never bothered......I wish now I had kept a few bits." Bernard had the impression that the box had to be raised slightly to accommodate the new locking associated with the frame, although there is no visual evidence of this from photographs. It is likely that the floor was instead raised inside the box as there was a step up from the door. Shortly after installation, of course, the new frame had to be inspected by the Ministry of Transport and a special train was laid on. The inspection at Welford went fine, but elsewhere on the branch it was not a good day as another train managed to run through the closed level crossing gates at Bockhampton near Lambourn.

A trespasser, or the ganger walking his length towards Newbury, or even someone with a Walking Permit - see page 27. We will never know, although the lack of a hammer or any other tools across the shoulder makes the latter more likely. The location is Speen cutting just south of the station and the site of much instability of the formation for some years. In the distance can be seen the bridge taking the railway under the Bath Road. It was here, on gradients as steep as 1 in 60 allied to the sharp curvature, that down trains, both steam and diesel hauled would often struggle for adhesion.

never once did one end up in the pot this way. Working the opposite shift to Edith at Speen was Don Uzzell, whilst a relative, Gordon Uzzell, was the Newbury based Relief Signalman, who would cover Welford when either Bernard, or his opposite number Charlie Marshall was absent. The late turn Porter at Speen was also responsible for lighting the lamps at West Fields Halt.

The trackwork on the branch was maintained by three gangs. Their areas of responsibility were, Newbury to Boxford, Boxford to Great Shefford, and Great Shefford to Lambourn. The gangers in charge were respectively, Mr Wootton, Bob Hopkins, and Mr Sampson. Each would be responsible for walking their 'length' daily, checking for worn or damaged fittings, oiling when necessary, as well as noting where work needed to take place. Summer time would see the gangers walking the length twice each day, as the keys holding the track secure were more likely to become dislodged, as the rails expanded in the heat.

Bernard recalled particularly the winter of 1953 / 1954 and especially January time when snow fell. He would normally ride his motorcycle to work from his home in Newbury but recounted that the snow on the roads came up to the footrests on his motorcycle and, during the journey from Newbury, he only met one other vehicle and that was when nearly at Welford. After that, and for a week whilst the snow persisted, Charlie and Bernard agreed to an unofficial swapping of shifts, where they would alternate between early and late turns, so that they could stay in the warm, sleeping in the box overnight.

Stores for the station and signal box, namely dusters, polish and of course stationary, would be delivered from Lambourn as required. Coal for the signal box stove was only provided once a year and was, of course, never enough. Often the loco crews would oblige by kicking a lump or two off the engine although at other times Bernard admits , "...we would borrow it from wagons destined for Lambourn".

Early shift was supposed to start at 06.50 am,

although Bernard admits himself he was often late. Whatever time he arrived his first task was to reach for the box key, 'hidden' by a nearby telegraph pole and then 'open' to Newbury West. Until he did and a token was released, the first empty train could not travel towards him. A few minutes later, around 7.00 am, he would 'open' to Lambourn, obtaining a token with the consent of the Lambourn man to allow the train to proceed to the terminus. There were now a few minutes when, if necessary, the stove could be stoked up. The empty train - usually of course a diesel - would pause only briefly at Welford, just sufficient time to exchange the token, although very occasionally there might be some paperwork, a new timetable, poster, or other notice handed to him by the guard as the empty passed through.

Before the train returned at around 8.23 a.m. as the first service to Newbury from Lambourn, several passengers would have arrived. These were mainly schoolchildren but as they had season tickets there was no booking to be done for them. Although there was a corrugated waiting room on each platform, several passengers would instead wait inside the signal box, totally against regulations of course, but the normal practice on the branch. A convenient wooden bench was located at the south end of the box.

When on late shift, Bernard would often be visited by some of his motorcycle friends. Indeed, on one occasions there were no fewer than 24 motorcycles present. Having a motorcycle himself was useful in other ways, such as the occasion a passenger, Joan Stroud, left her ticket on the train and Bernard chased the service as far as Speen to retrieve it. One of Bernard's duties was to ring the long term resident porter at Boxford, Arthur Smith and advise him whenever a train left Welford Park heading south. Arthur would always answer 'Yep' on the phone, and is recalled as wearing brown boots and always having his trousers at half-mast.

Being set in a rural community, traffic dealt with at Welford Park was limited. Passenger numbers came from service personnel at the nearby air-base, whilst women from

SCENES FROM A SIGNAL BOX - 2

Top left - Bernard complete with 'Velocette Mac'. He has owner the same machine, LCG 810, for over 50 years and in 2008 had just 52,000 miles recorded. It was built as a show bike - hence the extra chrome. Notice the dent on the silencer, caused Bernard recalls, when he clipped a kerb in London with a girlfriend on the back. The view was taken outside the little Booking-Office at Welford.

Top right - James ?, and Johnnie Mitchell, the latter the assistant lineman having a break inside the signalbox. The bench would sometimes be moved around and then it would be the signal box booking desk that was placed against the window.

Lower left - Lengthman Yohan Haigh - always known as 'Hans', a German who came to England in the 1940s and stayed to work on the railway. Recalled as an excellent worker, he is seen here unloading coal from a wagon into the signalbox bunker. Hans later took a course on British railway working, coming second in the whole of the country. He was awarded a prize - an all expenses trip to - Germany! (The propped wagon door will be noted, strictly against the rules but far more convenient.)

the local area were the other regular travellers - usually for shopping in Newbury. Bernard recalled that if they waited in the signal box their topics of conversation could be wide and varied....!

Goods and freight traffic was equally limited, although there were some regular and loyal customers. One was Millers Nursery and another school trunks for the children of Dr Scott. At Speen where traffic was equally restricted, Roy Flitter would sometimes deliver local items between trains using the station hand truck. Then there was the 'Watercress Man' from Stockcross, who would bring 20-30 baskets to the station to send on. Despite having his local station, which was un-staffed and he would prefer to come to Welford instead. Very occasionally a horse box, would arrive on the back of a Lambourn bound train intended for Diana Dodd. It would need to be placed in the siding at the station. Bernard recalled one occasion when this occurred and the horse box was one of two attached to the rear of the diesel. The crew simply uncoupled the required vehicle leaving it standing in the platform before running around and then gently pushing the horse box into the siding. They then reversed back out and finally continued on their way towards Lambourn. All this with passengers for stations up the valley still on board. (Bernard also admits he never mastered the use of a shunting pole. Others would whip a coupling on or off in no time, Bernard though always went between the vehicles instead).

Possibly the most unusual piece of traffic ever dealt with at Welford Park was a rhino horn mounted on a plinth, consigned from Major Archer Houblon. In an attempt at some form of protection in transit Bernard recalls that it was covered in sacking. The recipient is not recorded.

Bernard had another duty so far as Major Archer Houblon was concerned on a far sadder occasion. He recalls receiving a telephone call from Edith McCartney to inform him that the Major had died and would he 'go and tell them in the big house'.

In later years both passenger and goods traffic increased considerably for a time, following upon the expansion of RAF Welford. Service personnel often arrived in large numbers with just a few minutes to spare before a train was due to depart. The men would be clutching Travel Warrants which had to be converted into railway tickets. On one occasion, around the time the nearby base changed from being RAF Welford to USAF Welford, 30 men arrived in this fashion.

But most of the time at Welford it was a quiet life. The local carrier would sometimes call - there were several carriers who worked in the valley whilst there was also time to tend and admire the roses which grew together with violets and wild strawberries. Indeed, the fertile river valley produced a veritable display at times, including bluebells and snowdrops. Speen also had an equally dazzling display of Chrysanthemums whilst Tom Liddiard's station gardens at East Garston won several prizes in the annual railway competitions.

In between trains there might be the occasional poster to change, a glue pot being kept for this purpose. Bernard would also spent time chatting to the crews of trains, recalling two regular passenger guards in particular, Bill Holden and Fred Davis. Bill was always a happy man, whilst Fred was sometimes to be found in the 'Lamb' Public House during the layover at Lambourn. Goods guards were normally from Newbury, but there was no regular individual on this duty.

Each day the takings were placed in a small leather pouch which would in turn be put in the travelling safe. This was sent first to Lambourn, at which point the figures would be assimilated into the takings for the whole branch with the money all being sent from there to Newbury, usually by the mid-afternoon train. The cash-bag was returned to Welford later. In addition to cash, collected tickets, as well as details of tickets issued, warrants and goods details / receipts were included.

On Thursday each week, Stan Knapp, the Lambourn Station master, who supervised all the traffic department staff on the branch, would travel to Newbury to collect the wages. On his way back he would lean out of the window of the carriage passing out the wages. Bernard recalls Stan always had cigarette ash down the front of his waistcoat. If Charlie was unable to cover the opposite shift and likewise if there was no reliefman available, Bernard recalls having to work a double shift of up to 16 hours. Obviously this was overtime. His wages for the whole of 1956 being £473.10 s 5d gross, an average of just over £9 2s 0d a week.

Bob Sullivan, the Newbury District Inspector, has been mentioned earlier, but what has not been stated is that one of the DI's duties was to regularly check on the signalman in his district. This included not just the main line around Newbury, but also the Winchester and Didcot lines as well as the two signalboxes at Welford Park and Lambourn. Fortunately the men worked together whenever a visit was pending, as Mr Sullivan would also have to travel by train for his visits. There might then be a telephone call on the omnibus circuit that linked Newbury West and Welford Park. Bill Goodall at Newbury West keeping Bernard informed in his usual Berkshire drawl.

Bob, though, would rarely come to Welford direct. Preferring instead to alight at Boxford and walk the 1½ miles on the track, studying the flora and fauna. Upon arrival at Welford he would slope down in the 'box chair and first ask a few railway related questions, as he was required to do. After that, the remainder of the conversation was on his favourite subject, nature, and what he might have seen on his travels around the district. Possibly in the conversation he may have brought up the time some porters were attempting to move a trolley over the board crossing connecting the main platforms at Newbury. This was struck by the engine of the up 'Cornishman'. Fortunately no derailment occurred, although the contents of the trolley - flower seeds, were scattered over a considerable distance between Newbury and the Racecourse station. It did produce a wonderful display alongside the lineside the following year.

SCENES FROM A SIGNAL BOX - 3

Upper left - Lengthman Yohan Halch and John ?, both from the permanent way gang who covered Welford.

Top right - Two friends of Bernard's caught on camera at Welford during a 'quiet time'. At the top of the post is Dave Page, with Bernard's brother Jim on the ground, neither of whom were railwaymen. The post itself is of course for a Tilley lamp, which the late turn signalman would affix and then wind to the top as necessary. The Tilley lamps were kept in a corrugated lamp hut behind the signal box. Bernard and his colleagues were also responsible for cleaning and refilling the signal lamps at Welford which they attended to weekly.

Lower left - Charlie Marshall, Bernard's opposite number in the Signal Box. Although strictly against regulations, it was the practice at Welford Park to finish late shift as soon as the last train had departed for Newbury, rather than wait for it to arrive at its destination and receive 'Train out of Section'.

Lower right - The goods yard area depicted in its usual quiet state. For many years there had been a loading gauge across the siding but this was accidentally demolished by a delivery lorry and was never replaced. Bernard recounts, "...it was rotten anyway."

Welford Park - passenger bookings, August 1945	£	s	d
August 1st		16	11½
August 2nd		16	2
August 3rd	2	17	0½
August 4th / 5th	68	11	2
August 6th	1	3	9
August 7th	2	0	2½
August 8th		17	6
August 9th	2	8	3
August 10th	1	11	2½
August 11th / 12th	18	0	7½
August 13th	1	17	0
August 14th		11	11
August 15th / 16th	2	3	4½
August 17th	3	12	6
August 18th / 19th	20	3	5
August 20th	2	8	2
August 21st	1	14	10½
August 22nd	2	18	3
August 23rd	2	19	6½
August 24th	3	9	3½
August 25th / 26th	15	8	3½
August 27th		17	0½
August 28th		16	8
August 29th	1	8	8
August 30th	2	14	7
August 31st	3	11	0
	£165	17	5½

Above - Inside Welford Park signal box sometime after 1954. Charlie Marshall is seen in the background, Alan Marshall was visiting . The various notices, seats and paraffin lamps will be noted. A GPO outside line was also provided, Boxford 223, although the staff admit this was abused at times. There were also the more usual railway 'omnibus' telephone circuit.

Charlie Marshall, departed Lambourn for promotion to signalman at Welford Park and for the obvious reason of obtaining more money. He recalls cycling to work the six miles each way from his home at Lambourn and, after learning the 'box, was 'passed out' by the Newbury District Inspector, Bob Sullivan. As was the custom at the time, he had also to then be seen by Chief Inspector Honeybun at Paddington. Charlie does not recall much of the interview itself, but does remember that he was served a cup of tea in the railway canteen at Paddington, which contained a fly floating in the top.

It is rare to find photographs of the p/way staff at work and these two views from the early 1950s were most welcome. They depict the Welford Park gang with their push trolley, about to set off on weed killing duty. The same men are seen in both views and in the top view are recorded as (left to right); 'Hans' who lived at Boxford, on the trolley - Charlie Robbins who came from Bagnor, Lance Knight from Easton, and Jack Hobbs from East Garston. These were four of the six men in the Welford gang, the others being Bob 'Hoppy' Hoskins the Ganger and Jim Gasson who lived at Weston. Jim was a former welter-weight boxer and as such had considerable strength. This he would demonstrate on occasions by carrying a sleeper on each shoulder for a distance of about 200 yards.

Two further gangs of men looked after the tracks and engineering on the line. At Lambourn were four men, Alf Sampson - Ganger, assisted by Ted Gibbons, Sammy Sargeant and Charlie Mathews. At Speen were three men, known now only by their surnames, Messrs Chandler, Cripps and Stroud.

Opposite left - Charlie Marshall (left) and his Lambourn replacement, Alan Marshall posed against the road vehicle loading bank at Welford Park. It was perhaps ironic that Charlie lived near Lambourn and yet came to work at Welford whilst Alan came from Wickham, not far from Welford, and yet went to work at Lambourn. Charlie remained a regular signalman at Welford until 1958, when he took a position on the relief staff based at Newbury. Whilst on the LVR, although at the time he was not on duty, he recalled the occasion when the 8.00 a.m. from Lambourn, steam hauled and consisting of two coaches, jumped the track between Bockhampton and Eastbury leaving three of the four coach bogies off the rails. The cause was the rails having spread under the train. On another occasions some children were reported as having stolen the keys to the office at great Shefford. Nothing was taken, just the keys themselves.

All photos Charlie Marshall Collection

Above - No 1335 near Lambourn on 10th February 1940. On the opposite page Ray and Eric Hobbs recall various stories of the line during the war including, "...two large steam engines, pulling eight to ten carriages, chugging up the valley." Services such as these were likely to have had a pair of 'Dean Goods' or similar motive power.

S H Pearce Higgins

Left - Railway workers at East Garston in 1926. Left to right, Joe Green, Albert Barratt, Tom Liddiard and Willam Palmer. Tom Liddiard at least would remain on the railway for many years, being in charge of East Garston station up to the time of closure. The other three men are probably from the permanent way gang and would have been based at Lambourn. Joe Green is recalled as being able to cure warts, as if my magic and by touch alone.

Ray and Eric Hobbs - reminisce

Ray - "I recall early days of the Lambourn Valley Railway when on Thursdays, Cattle Market day and Street Market, the train was full to capacity on reaching Newbury Station.

"During World War 2 on Saturday afternoon lots of people used the train to go shopping in Newbury, they were full then as well.

"At weekends the trains were made up of a steam engine and sometimes two or even three carriages. Then again the Saturday evening train was also packed to capacity - local lads and service personnel who were billeted in the area, going to the cinema and pubs of course.

"Sometimes on the return journey fights would break out on the train resulting in the Military Police attending the last train at weekends. The last train from Newbury on Saturday night always left at 10.15 pm, right on time.

"The valley saw lots more traffic during the war years, at first due to British troop movements and later when America came into the war there were lots more troop trains going through with American G.I.s. Most of these trains were during the night. Troop trains generally consisted of two large steam engines pulling eight to ten carriages chugging up the valley. On certain inclines, like the one by East Garston, some trains would slip and slide on wet or greasy rails. We often wondered if they would make it through Eastbury cutting. Also, munitions trains would go through East Garston loaded with Personnel Carriers and Bren-gun Carriers, lorries guns - etc. All of this was unloaded at the Dock siding on Lambourn Station. Most of the troops were based in the Lambourn, Membury area, some at Ashdown and some at Ramsbury.

"I will now recall a couple of true stories about the last train leaving Newbury for Lambourn on Saturday evenings during the war.

"One local chap told me that on the way home in the train a fight broke out in the carriage where he was sat and he climbed up onto the luggage rack to get out the way but so missed East Garston station instead going through to Lambourn. Another local chap told me he bought a pair of shoes in Newbury and got off the last train at East Garston leaving the shoes on the train. He waited for the train to come back from Lambourn, but the late train was never scheduled to stop, instead running empty, so he got to the platform and waved a torch as it approached. Much to his surprise the driver did stop but it was nearly at School Lane bridge. He ran down the track but alas his shoes were missing.... .

"You just might be interested in a few of the names of the Drivers and Guards of the steam engines that came over the Valley railway. I recall a George Bedows, Rolly Ayres and Bert Portsmouth, all drivers. The guards of the trains were a Fred Davies, Bill Olding, Dick Tongate and many more.

"My father worked on the Permanent Way as Sub-Ganger for quite a few years - on the Welford length. In the winter months if fog came down in the evening, he had to cycle to Welford and walk the line putting down detonators to let the drivers know where they were approaching the stations. Some Sundays he would cycle to Newbury to join the relaying gangs on the main line, working all day putting in new rails and getting home late in the evening. The railway used to take the men from the branch lines to help on Sundays when there was less traffic around."

Eric recalled watching the goods train shunting trucks in East Garston goods yard, mainly on Saturday afternoons. The trucks were loaded with coal and farming material and would run into the siding on their own when shunted. He also remembered when in the church choir, listening to the sermon and hoping to hear the 7 o'clock train go by, knowing then it would soon be time to come out on a Sunday evening. When the service did finish the train to Newbury might still be in the station. If it had extra carriages and box vans on, the train would not clear the gates so they had to wait until it moved off. Eric recalled seeing cattle being unloaded at East Garston, which were then put in an adjacent field to wait collection by the farmers. Bungalows are now built on the field.

A two coach train at Great Shefford awaiting departure to East Garston. As has been described before, the rearmost coach is a former 'Toplight' slip vehicle now downgraded for branch line use.

Understandably views of the WW2 period are limited. To be fair the branch only played a restricted role in wartime traffic, although some workings and incidents did occur - see the reminiscences of Ray and Eric Hobbs on page 69. Indeed it was subsequent to conflict that Welford would be developed for munitions, as described in the next chapter. Meanwhile, No 18 is seen in Speen cutting on 19th June 1940 making its way north towards Lambourn. The introduction of the railcar had resulted in two steam turns being abolished one of which had regularly involved a former Cambrian Railways 0-6-0, by now GWR No 908. The introduction of the diesel no doubt contributing to its withdrawal from service in December 1938. Shortly after the photograph was taken No 18 and indeed all the railcars, were withdrawn from service, but subsequently reinstated due to motive power shortages.

At this stage in the conflict there had been no reports of enemy action affecting Berkshire although a record of the period from 1st July 1940 to June 1944 reveals a number of air raids occurred. Amongst those near to the Lambourn line were;

2- 9-1940	*Great Shefford. 1.02 am - 8 (small) H.E. dropped.*
1-10-1940	*Lambourn 5.05 am - 2 H.E. at Baze Farm.*
25-10-1940	*Lambourn 11.42 pm—3 H.E. north east of village near Trubbs Farm.*
28-11-1940	*Stockcross 10.40 pm - 2 H.E. 70 yards from Home Farm and 30 yards from iron bridge (GWR) Damage to houses, telephone wires and two horses killed.*
18– 4-1941	*Stockcross 2.20 a.m. 2 H.E. Window broken.*
6- 7-1942	*East Garston. Fragments of a German photoflash bomb picked up in a field, believed to have been dropped on 25-6-1942.*
23– 4-1943	*Lambourn 11.00 pm 2 H.E. in a field near Stancombe Farm.*

Finally, and although not related directly to the LVR, there was one incident of a V1 landing in a cornfield one mile north of Shaw village, at 3.18 am on 27-6-1944. Slight damage and one casualty - Mr Rowles (Farmer) who was blown out of bed.

DECLINE AND REVIVAL COMBINED

A case for closure of the Lambourn line came early in the days of British Railways. The first mention appeared in official correspondence dated 31st July 1950, which considered two options, complete closure and withdrawal of passenger services only. The latter was under the 'Integration of Transport' policy, whereby a duplication of services, viz rail and road, between the same two points would see one of these curtailed. In theory it was a laudable proposal, although, and as has been found so many times later, both road and rail have their advantages and disadvantages, neither able to totally successfully take over the operation of the other.

At this stage the papers were an internal Western Region discussion document, but it might also be worth mentioning, that to have even reached this stage, pressure being exerted to cut costs long before the well documented days of Dr Beeching. Whilst out of context here, it should also be mentioned that if this discussion was taking place re-Lambourn, it might be reasonably assumed it was also applicable to any number of other Western Region branch and lesser routes.

A potential alternative was to look at means of reducing operating costs and here discussion centred on the removal of the Lambourn bay at Newbury and recovery of the signal boxes at Welford Park and Lambourn, with points 8 and 15 (the run-round loop) at Lambourn being controlled by Ground Frame released by token. Similar arrangements were suggested at Welford Park, but here there is reference to the points being unlocked by keys on the train staff.

By 1951 the correspondence bundle is suggesting the influence of the Air Ministry in the proceedings, although in October of that year closure was still being considered, as witness, a detailed report entitled 'Integration of transport - Lambourn Branch'.

The full costs of operating the line were also given as far as the traffic department were concerned, which amounted to £5,213 per annum. The Lambourn Station Master at the time (Mr Knapp) earning £423 p.a., with the remaining costs attributable to 3 clerks, 4 signalmen, 5 leading porters, 2 porters and 3 lad porters. At Newbury costs involved in working the line in staff wages amounted to £1,586. The population of the catchment areas of the railway was given as 5,882, of which 1,168 were stated to be within the area of Newbury West Fields and 2,316 at Lambourn.

Goods traffic for 1950 was given as 17,571 tons of general merchandise forwarded and received, 5,996 tons of coal and 21 wagons of livestock. The general merchandise included grain, sugar beet and potatoes. Outwards, hay, straw and manure were forwarded, whilst fertilisers and grain was also received. 9,500 tons of the grain was moved was on behalf of the Ministry of Food, sent to and from Lambourn from whence it was transported by road for storage at the former Membury airfield.

The railway situation was hardly helped when it was stated that the train fare was almost double the corresponding bus fare between Newbury and Lambourn and even the cheap day railway tickets exceeded the road fare, 1/6d against 1/4d.

It was as if the decision makers were making a case to convince themselves closure was justified, as they naively stated that although in 1950 116 horses arrived at Lambourn and 114 were sent out, Paddington considered the trainers would prefer to take delivery of their horses at main line stations such as Newbury and Didcot. The fact such would involve a road journey from Lambourn to the railhead and it might even be appropriate to continue by road appears not to have been considered.

In the event of complete closure, goods, could be similarly dealt with, road haulage undertaken from Lambourn to the railhead at either Newbury or, in the case of grain destined to and from Membury, via Hungerford. Again there was a vast under estimate of the practicalities, as once the goods were on the road for some miles there would be an obvious reluctance to incur trasnshipment, whilst the roads in the area were hardly ideal for even the smaller vehicles of the period. Understandably, it was admitted that movement costs for goods by rail to and from Lambourn were in favour of the railway, compared with transport by road,

Economically, the total estimated gross expenditure on running trains on the Lambourn branch was given as £39,896 p.a. whilst, if services were withdrawn, there would be a saving to the Western Region of £31,713. The same document gives what are stated to be the receipts obtained, goods at £31,277 whilst passenger and parcels bookings amounted to £4,961.

A traffic census was also carried out, covering the week Monday 28th August to Saturday 2nd February 1950. This detailed passengers joining and alighting at each station, for every service between Newbury and Lambourn in either direction. The results revealed that the most patronised service in the down direction was the 4.15 pm from Newbury with a maximum of 60 persons and the least the 9.25 am from Newbury with just 2. The average, however, was in the order of just 17. In the reverse direction the most used was the 12.40 pm from Lambourn with a maximum of 78 passengers and the least the late evening service on Saturday, departing the terminus at 8.45 pm with just one passenger. Ironically this person alighted at the next

BRITISH RAILWAYS
(WESTERN REGION)

NEWBURY MICHAELMAS FAIR

FRIDAY, OCTOBER 14th

HALF-DAY EXCURSION TICKETS

will be issued
to

N E W B U R Y

FROM	RETURN FARES (Third Class)	
	s.	d.
Lambourn	1.	6.
Eastbury Halt	1.	6.
East Garston	1.	3.
Great Shefford	1.	0.
Welford Park		9.
Boxford		9.
Stockcross & B.		6.
Speen		3.

Children under Three years of age, Free;
Three and under Fourteen years of age, Half-fare.

AVAILABLE AS FOLLOWS:-

FORWARD

By the 10.40 a.m.,
12.40 p.m., 3.10 p.m.
and 6. 5 p.m. trains
from Lambourn.

RETURN

By any train
leaving Newbury
at or after
2. 0 p.m. the
SAME DAY.

NOTICE AS TO CONDITIONS.- These tickets are issued subject to
the conditions of issue of ordinary passenger tickets where
applicable and also to the special conditions as set out in
the Ticket, etc. Regulations, By-Laws and General Notices.
Luggage allowances are as set out in these general notices.

SPECIAL LATE RETURN SERVICE

A special late train will leave Newbury at 10.15 p.m.
calling at all stations to Lambourn except Newbury, West
Fields and Eastbury Halt.

Further information will be supplied on application to
Stations, Agencies or to Mr. C.W. POWELL, Divisional Superintendent, Paddington Station, W. 2.; or Mr. C. FURBER,
Commercial Superintendent, Paddington Station, W. 2. (Telephone: Paddington 7000, Extension "Enquiries", 8. 0 a.m. to
10. 0 p.m.).

K. W. C. GRAND,
Chief Regional Officer.

Paddington,
October, 1949.

radically alter the fortunes of the line for the subsequent two decades. This appears in a memorandum from the WR General Manager, K W C Grand at Paddington, dated the 29th October. The recipient is not stated, but by implication was the Air Ministry.

"In regard to your letter of the 8th August in connection with the provision of private sidings to serve the Air Ministry depot at Welford Park, it will be observed from the fourth paragraph of the Memorandum of Meeting held at Paddington on the 29th June last, that so far as the Operating department is concerned, the site chosen by the Air Ministry was arranged without the usual prior consultation with the Railway Authorities, and has resulted in presenting an operating commitment which was economically out of proportion to the tonnage of traffic to be moved". The earlier memo has not been located.

Clearly, then departments at Paddington were seemingly running two parallel yet diverse proposals, one for closure and the other for expansion, neither, it seemed being made aware of the other. Indeed, it was not until shortly after this that there appears to be a combining of resources, as it was mentioned that by 1951 the gross receipts were now £41,780 for goods and £13,215 for passengers. These figures were considerably above what had been stated as branch revenue just a year or so earlier and it is

station at Eastbury whereupon the train continued empty as far as Boxford where one passenger joined to travel through to Newbury.

Behind the scenes, though, it would appear that whilst one department at Paddington was making a case for closure, which realistically might well have reached an obvious conclusion, elsewhere at Paddington the higher echelons were engaged in secret discussion that would

obvious that such an increase in traffic was hardly likely to have occurred through natural means. The obvious conclusion must be that those promoting closure had managed to massage the earlier figures to promote their case. Indeed, it was later confirmed that the previously stated passenger revenue did not include ticket revenue for through bookings beyond Newbury and likewise in the reverse direction.

It appears that there was also a hope that the Air Ministry might take over maintenance of the branch between Newbury and Welford, although this would imply that public services would have been unlikely to have been continued, whilst there is no mention of the fate of the section north of Welford. Conversely, it was also stated that a railhead at Welford would be likely to generate goods in the order of 1,000 tons daily and a corresponding increase in passenger numbers.

Here, then, is also another raft of questions. 1,000 tons of goods - the equivalent of 100 contemporary 4-wheel wagons, surely not from general traffic? This figure must have included the anticipated levels of material from the Air Ministry. Possibly also the railway considered Welford would be similarly used by military personnel. The latter, at least, was a realistic assumption although in practice the number of service personnel travelling by train was never considerable nor regular.

Evidently, the General Manager at least, had now conceded that closure was impossible, due to what was obviously a commitment to afford private siding facilities. In a memorandum, dated 21st April 1952, he almost reluctantly confirmed, "...it has become necessary to postpone indefinitely consideration of the proposals.....to withdraw the passenger and goods service.....under an integrated scheme." Two days later, approval was also given to embark on brush repainting of the stations on the branch, by contract for £1,000, a matter that had been on hold dependent upon the result of the closure proposals. The simple matter of painting would be the subject of further discussion later.

The actual connection and sidings at Welford, similarly the alternative proposal for a loop connection from the Air Ministry site back into the line at Great Shefford, have been mentioned in the original book and will not be detailed again here. Suffice to say that the plans finally approved by the Western Region and the Air Ministry were apparently concluded by the autumn of 1952 and on the 22nd October, there is mention of the amount of material that will be required, just for the new siding accommodation at Welford;

420 tons of rails
241 tons of chairs
152 cwts fishplates
5,386 sleepers
1,440 cu ft crossing timbers
11,640 keys etc.

A undated memo from around this time also paved the way for heavier engines to use the line, a situation no doubt hastened by the impending new sidings. Accordingly, 'Yellow' engines could now use the line subject to a general 20 mph speed limit. This from this time on, locomotives of the 22xx and 57xx types would be seen. The days of the railcars alone were coming to an end whilst the remaining 'Dean Goods' type were nearly all by now withdrawn.

Paddington had studied the existing timetable and concluded that there were at the present eight spare paths

Opposite page - Excursion traffic for 1949. Compared with the more usual properly printed handbills this was a crude, but nevertheless valiant attempt to attract traffic.

This page - Goods receipts for items sent from Welford Park in 1949 and 1950, still, of course, using GWR paperwork. The rural nature of the railway is exemplified by the produce on the top receipt, whilst below, the name of the consignor was of course synonymous with the railway and of course Welford Park itself.

available between Newbury and Welford. Allowing for 15 wagons being taken per trip, 840 tons daily could be dealt with. However, if passenger services were withdrawn, a further seven paths would became available, meaning that up to 225 wagons totally some 1,575 tons might be handled.

The relatively minor issue of the repainting reappears at this stage, as it was now realised that the apportioned cost of £40 to repaint Newbury West Fields Halt could hardly be justified in view of the limited number of passengers who used the facility. Unlike the other stopping places, nowhere in the passenger count is West Fields referred to separately. Consequently complete closure was recommended. At Stockcross & Bagnor, annual income was roughly equivalent to annual maintenance with five passengers joining and three arriving daily. The memo felt that local opposition would be aroused here if closure were contemplated at that time and that painting should be carried out. A warning for the future came with the rider that closure could be considered at a later date in the event of further renewals or expenditure.

Closure was still very much in mind in early February 1953, when it was stated that every effort must be made to reduce costs, although there was some concern that by taking action the attractiveness of the service might be affected. Amongst the matters then being considered were making Boxford unstaffed, so saving the £300 pa wages of the one woman porter (Edith McCartney) employed.

Passengers from Boxford might obtain tickets on the diesel car and parcels might be delivered by the zonal lorry from Newbury. It was sated that, during 1952, 45 wagons were despatched from Boxford, mainly hay and grain, whilst 46 wagon loads were received. The incoming traffic consisted of fertilisers, seed potatoes in the early part of the year and 2-3 loads of general goods. Goods traffic was generally seasonal.

Another area looked at for economy was the staffing of Speen. Although here it was accepted that the lad porters employed could not be replaced by a female crossing keeper, who at the time would have been paid less than a man. Indeed, it was accepted that it would be difficult to secure the services of someone for the whole day's service, 8.20 a.m. to 7.40 p.m,. whilst the buildings at Speen could not be adopted as accommodation for a crossing keeper. Clearly whoever made this suggestion at Paddington had no idea of the actual facilities that existed.

A note of 26th March 1953 commented that three guards were used to cover the services on the line and, in addition to train duties, also issued tickets to passengers joining at the unstaffed halts of West Fields, Stockcross and Eastbury by means of a "rather cumbersome ticket case.....it will not be possible to add to this". It was suggested an alternative could be the introduction of either printed 'Bell Punch' tickets or even better a 'Bell Punch' machine as supplied to the Thames Valley Traction Company, the working of which was such that it printed the required amount on each ticket, dependant upon the fare stage. 'Bell-Punch' type tickets were indeed introduced at a later stage.

See illustrations on page 81.

On the 7th May 1953 a formal proposal was made to withdraw goods services from Boxford, the population of which was 440. The principal traders using the station were stated as Mr. Snook, Mr. Wallis and also Johnson Bros who dealt in potatoes and fertilisers. Total goods dealt with at Boxford in 1952 was 574 tons, providing for £853 in receipts. Passenger bookings in 1951 were 3,636 tickets amounting to £209 8s.10½d, whilst in 1952 this had fallen to 3,083 tickets worth £205 15s 10½d. Clearly there were fewer tickets but proportionately of a greater value each. Parcels traffic, the figure for which was not stated, was additional. An average of 22 passengers used the trains daily, the heaviest usage being on Thursday and Saturday. An added factor contributing towards closure was that the buildings at Boxford were stated not to be in very good condition.

Meanwhile in June 1953, work was progressing on the sidings at Welford, the railway installing a water supply for the use of the contractor, W & C French Ltd.

Paddington, though, were still concerned over operating costs, as a June 1953 record afforded details of receipts for the intermediate branch stations compared with expenditure.

The figures given are interesting, for they would hardly bear out justification for the withdrawal of facilities at Boxford. Indeed if the case at Boxford was based on the above amounts, which are indeed very similar to those earlier, then with the exception of West Fields Halt all of the branch

	Annual Revenue	Annual Maintenance Costs
Newbury West Fields Halt	£ 17 5s 7d	£23
Speen	£157 18s 0d	£20
Stockcross & Bagnor	£126 11s 9d	£20
Boxford	£309 10s 1d	£20
Welford Park	£379 11s 4d	£40
Great Shefford	£831 2s 3d	£40
East Garston	£531 7s 3d	£20
Eastbury	£ 80 15s 6d	£20

stations were safe. What is interesting is that the greatest revenue was being accrued from the stopping places beyond Welford, yet this was also precisely the section of line that would be closed completely just a few years later.

Contemporary BR records would appear to confirm the above, for a note added to the above figures commented that there was justification in retaining staff at Welford Park, Great Shefford and East Garston. Boxford, though, was mentioned as having two leading porters employed. Earlier reports mention just the one and that as such it was

Early days in the new work at Welford Park. The view is a rather cruel enlargement from a section of a photograph although the point of interest here has to be the wagons and contractors vehicles in the yard. The building with the striped end is interesting, possibly provided as temporary accommodation for the contractor, Messrs French. It is also just possible to determine piles of pipes, whilst the open wagons also have their side doors open unusually on the wrong side to the yard hardstanding.

Work in progress alongside the original single line at Welford Park. The view is looking north, the 'down' direction, towards the station, one of the platforms of which may just be seen in the background. The lead from the single line towards what will be the exchange sidings behind the station has been installed. At this stage the boundary has been extended eastwards and the ground prepared for the single line that will run parallel for a short while. In consequence the bridge over a minor road will be extended.

Opposite top - Looking back over the new bridge towards the station The signal engineer has also been busy, the new bracket eventually to become the 'Down Outer Home' and 'Main to Air Ministry sidings Home'.

Opposite bottom - The new bridge in course of construction and as built alongside the original. Compared to the original 19th century metal structure, the new one uses the then preferred material of concrete. All the views in this sequence were taken sometime in 1953/4.

Above - The formation for the new line, running alongside the existing route just south of Welford Park. The bridge and signal referred to are just out of sight around the corner. The new line initially took a southerly course, before turning almost through 90° to head towards the camp. This was necessary due to the contours of the land, although it meant the route was far longer than if it had taken a direct path. Whether the latter was ever considered is not known. Suffice to say that the depth of the cuttings that would have been required may have rendered this impractical. Already the change of levels from the original branch will be appreciated. The exposed earthworks are in many ways similar to latter year motorway construction.

The original proposals for the military line envisaged a take off point 'near Boxford'. The exact spot was not stated. Later, after Welford had been decided upon, there was a suggestion that the exchange sidings be continued and connected into the branch beyond the station to afford run-around facilities. This was frowned upon as it would have meant MoD locomotives using BR track. There was also a suggestion that the camp line should continue from the base and connect into the branch again at Great Shefford. A cutting was evidently started within the base towards Great Shefford, but not proceeded with. The first discussions concerning the new line appear to have taken place between BR and the Ministry from mid 1951 onwards and were prefaced 'Secret'. At that time the likely traffic flow was estimated at ten trains daily which would mean doubling the intended holding facilities at Welford to accommodate 200 wagons. In the end this was not undertaken. The Western region motive power department were also concerned that whilst the Chief Civil engineer was prepared to pass the 22xx class for use on the line at a speed not exceeding 20mph, the amount of traffic envisaged would mean this class regularly working on the line, which could then mean that strengthening or reconstruction work would be required. In the event, of course, traffic flow never reached that forecast.

Top - The photographer has moved around the corner slightly. The original branch is running in the valley near the trees whilst the new line can be seen to have curved eastwards and gained height. At this stage the trackwork has yet to be ballasted, aligned and tamped. For cheapness ash ballast was used although this created drainage problems and led to the rotting of sleepers. The apparent haste in construction, never explained, has meant that the boundary fences have not even been completed. Subsequent formal operation of the military line would appear to have been the military equivalent of 'One Engine in Steam', although it is not known if a form of 'staff' was ever carried. Certainly there were never any signals, other than provided by BR at Welford Park itself.

Centre - Slightly further east this time. The end of the track seen in the top view may just be discerned in the distance. This and the lower view show the slight embankment provided at this point, which was again following a curved path. The presence of the hay ricks nearby, allied to the bleak background, may well indicate sometime in the period autumn to spring 1953/4. In later years the M4 motorway would traverse the valley to the left and it was this curved embankment that was visible on the high ground to the north of the motorway. Following closure of the line, the embankment was removed and the land returned to farm use. When operational, track maintenance was carried out by Ministry of Defence staff.

Bottom - By swinging the camera through 180°, we see the end of the embankment, but by now with track temporarily in position. As before fencing had yet to be added. The crossing was provided for the farmer whose land had been dissected and believed to have been retained whilst the railway was operational. It is not known whether any further crossings were built. Throughout the line leading to the base , the maximum gradient was 1 in 82 and the minimum curve 16 chains. A rise in level of between 150 and 160 feet was achieved in the 2½ miles between Welford Park station and the camp.

The deep cutting leading towards the camp, believed here looking west. Here the route passed through clay at one end and chalk at the other, resulting in a difficult formation for the engineers. It would appear that turf has been laid and that this is the task in progress. Was this for stability or even intended as some form of camouflage?

uneconomic. There was no problem at Stockcross or Eastbury, as both were unstaffed. At Speen there was a problem, as costs exceeded revenue, even though it was only two lads who were employed for the purpose of the level crossing.

Meanwhile, inflation resulted in estimates rising and the delay in awarding the painting contract meant that by the time the General Manager had finally given approval for this, the amount involved was £1,012 0s 11d. It was awarded to Messrs Fields of Reading. This did not include any work at Newbury West Fields Halt.

The question of lighting at the stations was evidently also discussed around this time but no details are given.

The survey of usage at Speen level crossing was referred to in the original book although some more details revealed that during normal station opening hours, 6.30 am to 7.30 pm, the crossing was used by:

The railway's intention to close West Fields Halt had reached the attention of the Newbury Town Council, as a letter was sent from Leslie Sutton, Town Clerk, protesting

	'Motors'	Cycles
Thursday 18-6-1953	219	184
Friday 19-6-1953	197	148
Saturday 20-6-1953	222	173

that, "...the Halt is of great convenience to business people and others who travel to Reading and London in the early morning, as the 8.41am train connects with the 8.52 am up train at Newbury main line station." A similar argument was made for the evening and also for those from Westfields who wish to travel to Newbury. They would now be forced to walk for 1 mile or get the bus into the Wharf and then change to a Lambourn bus.

Possibly to verify the figures sent by the Council Paddington conducted it's own survey of use. The results were that in the week ending the 11th October 1952, no passengers at all joined the first up train to Newbury throughout the whole week and just one arrived from Newbury on the last train on Saturday. Indeed total

Left - Diesel railcar No 18 leaving Welford for Lambourn, reportedly sometime in 1956. In the background No 3738 is in the platform having waited for the passenger train to clear the section south.

Norman Simmons / Hugh Davies NO228D

Opposite page - Bell Punch ticket for a single fare from Welford Park to Newbury on 23rd October 1959. Another example is seen in colour on page 37.

passenger usage for the week was 16 persons joining and 17 alighting. Whether these results were communicated to Mr Sutton is not reported, but the obvious result was a formal notice published in the *NEWBURY WEEKLY NEWS* for 6th August 1953 advising of the intended closure of the West Fields Halt.

Even so, it would appear the railway was still undecided, as one month later a further comment was made by Paddington to the effect that with normal maintenance the platform should last for 30 years but the shelter will need replacing in five. With no maintenance these times come down to five years and two years.

Whether the Lambourn branch was, for some reason, a special case is not clear, but it would appear that what should have been a relatively simple decision whether to close what was, in reality, a little used minor stopping place could not be taken other than by the General Manager. Consequently Mr Grand finally gave his decision on 8th October 1953, which confirmed the Halt could remain open with no maintenance, a further review to take place in two years time. Indeed, up to now it is still hard to determine if the various suggestions made by the WR were a genuine means of attempting to save operating costs, or steps to reduce revenue and so justify closure.

The decision to remove freight facilities from Boxford had by now also been made public, attracting protest once more from Newbury Town Council and also the local branch of the National Farmers Union. Once more Paddington capitulated and on 28th January 1954 it was agreed that, whilst Boxford would become an unstaffed halt, facilities for dealing with freight would be retained. Was it a case of seeing what might be reduced without protest? Assuming so, little had so far been achieved. Indeed, just after this, Paddington released the figures for traffic handled at Boxford during 1953. These revealed that 2,861

passengers were booked from the station, an average of around nine per day on weekdays, and contributing a revenue of £181 18s 0½d. 69 parcels were sent out, worth £22 5 0s 11d, whilst 395 were received. But none of this covered the cost of the one porter employed, whose annual wage bill was £436. It would have made total economic sense to remove that member of staff, but instead it was commented that Boxford may retain its goods facilities and the duties in connection with freight "...to be undertaken by a unit, (probably meaning a member of staff) from an adjacent station as required."

A similar situation was taking place at Speen, where rather than reducing costs, it was now almost the opposite, for on 17th March 1954 there was a proposal to spend £25 altering the wicket gates at Speen for the convenience of cyclists. This was considered necessary, '..bearing in mind the project at Welford Park," presumably the extra traffic anticipated. Shortly after this the cost had risen to £34 but without any definite decision being made. Instead a further survey of delays at the crossing was made. This time it appears to have concentrated solely on cyclists. The result was that during the survey period - when was not stated - 138 cyclists used the crossing, out of which two were delayed by one minute and a further three by two minutes.

We now revert to the situation at Boxford and the 'yes-no' decision to remove the porter. In reality, the indecision of Paddington should, be expected, bearing in mind the Newbury West Fields experience a little earlier. Finally, it appears that, on the 23rd June 1954, a decision was made to reduce Boxford to an unstaffed halt, although no implementation date was given. This might be expected to be an end of the matter, until a note of the 2nd August 1954 commented that due to unspecified accountancy difficulties the decision had been "postponed".

There is now another mention of lighting proposals, although once again the context is not stated. In the 'light' - pardon the pun of what would be reported shortly, it may even be that the lighting comments relate to how Boxford would be lit, if and when the porter were removed. The other unstaffed halts had lights that were lit and placed by a porter from a neighbouring station and then extinguished by the guard of the last train.

By the 14th January 1955 comment was made that the only stores to be returned from Boxford were a ticket case and standard parcels stamp label case. It was said they had still not been returned to the stores department at Swindon over two months later. The wooden office on the platform was being used by a member of staff, in view of the increased freight traffic which was passing at present.

Sometime after this, tickets ceased to be issue at Boxford, the train guard dealing with these instead. Possibly this was the time 'Bell Punch' type tickets were brought into use.

Next, on the 6th October 1955, an amazing internal memorandum emerged concerning the new sidings at Welford, which is best recounted in full:

"Squadron leader Cook - working with the American Forces - telephoned this afternoon in connection with explosives now being forwarded from Cairn Ryan, Scotland, to the American Unit at Welford Park. He stated that the traffic which is substantial, is passing at present to Newbury Station and collected from that point. He now learns that private siding facilities are in existence at Welford Park and asks whether it would be possible to arrange for reception of future traffic through the siding. As traffic is now in the process of loading at forwarding station, he requested a reply by telephone.......Squadron Leader Cook stated that the reason for the urgency is the fact that the American Forces are being involved in considerable expense by cartage from Newbury and it is necessary to put a stop to this unnecessary expenditure immediately, if in fact, direct railway facilitates are available. Promised Squadron leader Cook that immediate steps would be taken to ascertain he position regarding acceptance of this traffic. Gave Mr Bullock (Private Sidings) full details over the telephone."

Clearly neither the railway nor the military were communicating about the new facilities that were available. The results, though, were swift, as at 4.10 pm on the same day, a hand written note appeared after discussion with the District Goods Manager at Reading. It appeared that at Welford Park the military had refused to accept trains of munitions, as they themselves had no engine power and there was no road access to the military sidings at Welford. Indeed there never was. Even so, the latest munitions train arriving at Newbury was, in fact, diverted to Welford and subsequently unloaded into road transport at the BR goods siding alongside the main running line.

It would also appear that someone at Welford was

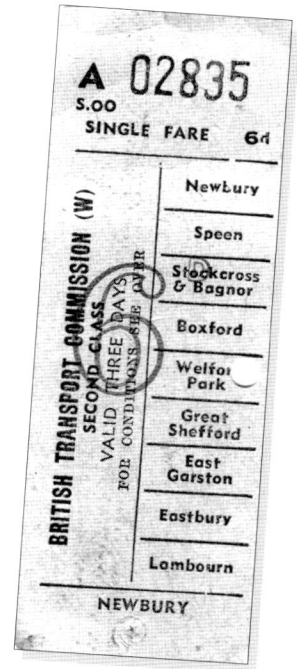

Typical of the branch services - off peak at least, in the 1950s. A locomotive and single coach, in this case 57xx class No 7708. The view is of course taken in the Lambourn bay at Newbury, the engine release crossover for which can also just be seen. Today the canopy still survives although the area occupied by the track has long been filled in and forms part of the station car-park. The road vehicle is in the same position as its compatriot on page 37.

MUNITIONS AT WELFORD

Thanks to the foresight of Welford Park Signalman, Charlie Marshall, it is possible to illustrate military traffic within the exchange sidings at Welford Park. As can be seen, there was no road access to this side of the station site although there is no record of civilian goods traffic ever having been handled at this point (although clearly the signal box coal supply was unloaded that way for convenience - see page 63) as has been referred to in the text. So far as the workings were concerned, traffic destined for the base would usually arrive in trainload form. It was then left for collection by the small diesel locomotive(s) from the base. Due to the gradients to the base, the locomotive was always at the lower end of the train in either direction, hence the need to keep one of the through lines clear, to allow the engine to arrive at the end of the train nearest the camera in the above view. Wagons from the camp would arrive at the sidings but sometimes needed to be sheeted before further onward transfer. It was on one of these occasions, when two BR men, Reg Hatter and Bert Nymms, both normally based at Great Shefford, were sheeting wagons, that an engine arrived from Newbury to collect a train and ran straight into the sidings at too fast a speed. To be fair Bernard, who was the duty signalman at the time, should not have had the road set into the yard and the signal lowered until the engine had come to rest, but for some reason, now long forgotten, everyone was a hurry on that day. The route was also set straight for the line of waiting loaded wagons. The result was that the engine was seen with its wheels spinning and then sliding as the driver desperately tried to stop in time. None of this was enough and there was a load bang, as a collision took place although fortunately nothing worse occurred. Bernard and his colleagues recall the American engines as being 'useless' both for pulling and as regards their braking ability. Consequently, it was not unknown for a BR engine to unofficially work traffic as far as the gates of the camp, likewise, on the journey back to the BR exchange sidings, a man would walk alongside pinning the brakes on the wagons due to the steep descent. Prior to the provision of the military line wagon loads of shells would be unloaded in the single goods siding and then taken to the camp by road. The bombs being unloaded by a portable crane, provided by the USAAF in the yard. This in itself was not without incident, such as when one fell off the crane and also when three 250 lb bombs fell off the low-loader lorry leaving Welford, but fortunately landed on soft ground. The cause was excessive speed on the part of the lorry driver. At Welford Camp itself there existed a kiln which was used to incinerate old ammunition. The noise of this popping and banging could be heard from the railway.

Form (left)

M.116).

BRITISH RAILWAYS

RECOMMENDATIONS OF SIGHTING COMMITTEE

MEETING HELD ON 14th January, 1957. AT WELFORD PARK. PLAN No

SUBJECT. Renewal and alteration to Signals.

NAMES & LEVER NUMBER OF SIGNALS	EXISTING No.4 Down Main Starting. No.15 Down Main to Siding.	PROPOSED No.4 Down Main Starting. No.15 Down Main to Siding.
PROFILE OF SIGNAL SHEWING (a) REPEATING e.g. AR LR ALR ASR ASLR SR SLR	NONE	NONE
(b) HEIGHTS ABOVE RAIL	16'6"	18'0"
(c) CENTRE OF POST TO RAIL	6'6"	6'6"
(d) SPACE BETWEEN RAILS		MECH NONE
(e) METHOD OF OPERATION	MECH NONE	
(f) TELEPHONE REQUIREMENTS		
(g) POSITION OF RAILS IN RELATION TO SIGNALS		
FOGGING PARTICULARS		
1 YARDS FROM SIGNAL BOX	6 yards	6 yards
2 YARDS FROM OUTERMOST HOME		
3 YARDS FROM OUTERMOST STARTING SIGNAL OF BOX IN REAR		
4 GRADIENT FROM DISTANT TO OUTER HOME		
5 MAX ALLOWABLE SPEED		300
6 MAX ATTAINABLE SPEED	300	
7 SIGHTING DISTANCE STOP / DISTANT	Yes	Yes
8 CAN SIGNAL BE SIGHTED FROM NEXT SIGNAL IN REAR?	Yes	None
9 ARE CATCH POINTS AFFECTED IF SO, STATE YARDS IN REAR OR AHEAD OF SIGNAL	None	None
10 POINT OF NEAREST POWER SUPPLY TO (a) SIGNAL BOX (b) SIGNAL	None	
11 NEAREST MILEPOST TO SIGNAL	6	6

REMARKS

209

THE ABOVE RECOMMENDATIONS PROPOSED BY:- FOR O.S. --- E.J.Sullivan. FOR M.P.S. --- B.R.Bettifer.
FOR S&T E --- W.J.Stark.
FOR C.E. --- R.Stevenson.

ITEMS 2,3,4,5 & 6 NEED ONLY BE COMPLETED FOR DISTANT SIGNALS

Report of the sighting committee at the time the wooden bracket comprising the Down Main Starting (No 4) and Down Main to Siding (No 15) signals were renewed at Welford Park, early in 1957. The replacement being a single tubular post and ground disc. In the same year, 1957, other alterations to the signals at Welford which were made included a metal post replacement for the Up Main Starting Signal (No 21). Slightly earlier, in 1954, the Down (fixed) Distant at Welford had been repositioned 75 yards further towards Newbury because of the new, bracket, outer home signals. Also in 1957, fixed distant signals were provided for trains in both directions, on the approach to the level crossing at East Garston and in the down direction, at least approaching Speen. This may well be in consequence of a number of run-throughs at the actual level crossings. Prior to this, there had been no signals of any sort on the approach to these level crossings

delivered a personal 'rocket', for immediately afterwards comes a note that the depot engine is now serviceable although, it was limited in power to working just four loaded vehicles at a time up the gradient to the depot.

On the 16th October 1955, what was then the first comment for some time concerning the new sidings and connection to the air base at Welford, appears, reiterating the earlier difficulties. It seemed that despite the Government, through the Air Ministry, having expended a considerable sum on the new sidings, new line and camp rail facilities, munitions traffic destined for Welford was not all moving by rail, Instead some traffic would still arrive by rail at Newbury and then be sent to Welford by road. The reason this time was that the Americans, who were then in charge of Welford, did not now have an engine, although they were hoping to have one in two months time! Maintenance of the military line was another issue and it appears that BR were approached to undertake all requisite track maintenance, both up to and within the depot site. BR, though, declined, citing staff shortages as the reason.

By 28th November 1955, over two years had elapsed since Newbury West Fields had last come up for discussion and Paddington sought permission to remove the shelter and platform, creating a slope and making good the fence. The estimate for this work was £90, although there would be a credit of £30 on materials recovered. The total bookings for West Fields in 1954 stated to have been just £8. It would also appear that, on the 18th October 1955, the condition of Newbury West Fields had drawn adverse comments from the Ministry of Transport Inspecting Officer. How this came about can only be surmised, and it may be that it was noticed when passing through to inspect the new signalling and connections at Welford Park.)

Once more, though, it was the General Manager who was called upon to make a decision and this time it was a common sense approach that, instead of commenting on individual stations, the line itself should be considered as a whole. Even so, on the 8th March 1956, final consent was at last given at Paddington to close West Fields, although it was not until 6th December in the same year that the Transport Users Consultative Committee sanctioned the closure. Newbury West Fields Halt thus finally ceased to operate as a stopping place from the 4th February 1957. It had been open just over 60 years.

Even so, references to West Fields would continue to crop up for some months. These included comments on the necessity for, positioning of and, of course, cost of whistle boards, now necessary as an occupation crossing existed at the Newbury end of the site. Then there was the cost of removing what was recoverable from the site and making it good. The estimates for both the latter also vary somewhat from those originally given, whilst the very last reference in the file to the stopping place appears in May 1957.

We now return again to the Air Ministry sidings, both at Welford and leading to and within the camp itself, likewise the provision of suitable motive power. On 23rd January 1958 there is mention of what was the obvious, using

Edith McCartney, watching a Newbury train departing from Speen. Reading loco crews were the regular men over the line at this time but even so this did not stop them from occasionally running through the various level crossing gates in darkness, fog, or having simply expected them to be open when they were not. It was probably the unfamiliarity of a Didcot crew on the by now curtailed Sunday service, that once led to them to demolishing all three sets of gates on a single trip, one Sunday in earlier years.

BR locomotives to shunt to and from the Camp at Welford. It was implied that, at some stage previously a trial using a BR locomotive had been carried out, but no other details were given.

The difficulties were obvious. From the sidings at Welford Park the new line was on a rising gradient of 1 in 80 for two miles, upon which the two diesel locomotives were incapable of operating satisfactorily. It was suggested that a 22xx would be suitable and that no spark arrestor would be required. The BR locomotive only take the wagons as far as the main sidings at the camp, from where the diesels would take over the final distance to the munitions store. Due to the gradients, the steam locomotive would be limited to 15 loaded wagons per trip but, even so, four trips per day were possible. Evidently, munitions loads of 60 wagons per day were at that time then commonplace as, by implication, if the arrivals were limited to 30 wagons per day, the existing diesels could in fact cope. For security purposes it was proposed that a USAF representative would travel on the loco, so a shunter/guard would not be required. The new arrangements were intended to start in February 1958, coinciding with the anticipated arrival of a monthly shipment from an unstated port. The 22xx locomotive would be supplied from Reading shed.

It was now back to the branch itself, more specifically its own future. Possibly this was a direct result of the General Manager's earlier comments, to view the route as a whole, which should have made for comfortable reading.

Despite thus apparent operating surplus, Paddington had decided to include a reference to the fact that £51,550 would need be expended during the next few year, the vast majority (£50,000) on permanent way renewals and with lesser amounts on a hut, fencing and painting. Immediately, though, a question is raised over the impact, or otherwise the Air Ministry traffic was having on the line. Was this being carried free, at a notional charge, or

1956	Number of Passengers / parcels	£
Receipts Passengers	80,753	5,303
Receipts Parcels	7,174	2,257
Receipts Goods		40,467
Total Receipts		48,027
Less Operating Costs		26,875
Gross Profit		21,152

did the Western Region simply not apportion a correct proportion of costs to this traffic? Sadly the conclusion drawn, even at this stage, is that a decision had been made to close the line. The figures would be 'manipulated' and there was nothing anyone could do to prevent it.

A mention is made of an alternative 'lightweight diesel service being provided for most workings, with tickets issued by the guard. But surely here it was a question of reinventing the wheel. Had there not been a diesel service until quite recent times? The actual date the former GWR design railcars ceasing operating the branch is not completely certain but is believed to have been around 1955/56. As an aside, Chris Webb from Winchester recalls travelling on the BR type 'lightweight' diesel units used for the final services on the line between Newbury and Didcot. He recalls the destination blinds for these vehicles included Lambourn. As far is known, though, no diesel of this type ever worked through to Lambourn at this time.

Some notes were also made about cost savings through rationalisation, which included removal of the bay at Newbury, introducing 'train staff, one engine in steam' working between Welford Park and Lambourn and all staff posts to be abolished save for a Leading Porter at

In June 1958, a resume of the current staff situation of the branch, which included 2 occupation and 25 accommodation crossings, was as follows;		
Lambourn	Station Master - Class 2	Stan Knapp
	Clerk - Class 4	Mrs 'Lotty' Knapp
	2 Signalman - Class 4	Bill Mabberley and Jack Alexander
	Senior Porter	Basil (Bunny) Brown
	Junior Porters	David Rosier and Alan Marshall
East Garston	1 Leading Porter	Tom Liddiard
	1 Ordinary Porter	Bert Nymms
Great Shefford	2 Leading Porters	Reg Hatter and Arthur Smith
Welford Park	2 Signalman	Charlie Marshall and Bernard Smith
Speen	2 Junior Porters	Edith McCartney and Roy Flitter
Engineering Department **- see page 67**	2 Gangers	
	2 Sub-Gangers	
	2 Lengthmen	
(The names given are as accurate as possible)		

Lambourn and signalman at Welford. Even so, it was admitted that any such savings made would be negligible.

Where the naivety of the railway management of the time comes in, was to believe that even if a rationalisation of services took place, passengers and goods would simply make their own way to the nearest railhead and continue to use the service. This simply did not happen, or where it did it did not continue for long. It was a situation that applied equally to passenger and goods traffic.

It was thus clear that the Western Region was moving towards closure beyond Welford, whist Paddington were also confident to believe that racecourse traffic would now be dealt with at Newbury, although a sop was that the platform at Stockcross should be retained for special trains.

All freight would also be diverted to Welford Park, where additional yard accommodation would be provided. In connection with this, it was proposed to transfer the 20T cart weighbridge from Lambourn to Welford (the 12T weighbridge from Great Shefford would become redundant). Space would also be made available at Welford for the various coal merchants currently using Lambourn and East Garston, whilst Boxford, despite all the mutterings earlier, would continue to handle freight as before.

Whether this provision for additional freight at Welford meant within the new sidings, or an extension of the facilities on the single original goods siding at Welford is not certain. Possibly the latter, as there is no mention anywhere of laying down more sidings. The only extra work referred to was an additional building to be used as a weighbridge office at Welford, 20' x 10', which would cost

£2,450. It was proposed also that the safe at Lambourn Booking Office would be transferred for use at Welford Park.

It was noted that in addition to the existing railway facilities north of Welford becoming redundant and able to be sold, the station house at Lambourn would also become redundant.

Somehow Paddington managed to come up with a figure of £17,806 as an annual saving, were the line to be closed. The only way this appears to be justified was an approximate one third of the £51,000 cost of renewals, spread over three years.

The recommendation, then, was for the withdrawal of passenger services with the line to be abandoned between Welford Park and Lambourn.

Once again matters appear to reside in limbo, although in May 1959 the matter of closure was once again raised at Paddington and it was agreed that an up to date summer census should be carried out. It does not appear this was ever done, although, even if it had, one wonders if it would have conveniently ignored the peak morning and evening services used by schoolchildren during term time.

Closure plans were thus announced and the matter referred to the TUCC. This otherwise august body were evidently convinced by the railway's argument and, despite not holding their discussions until early October 1959 the result of their deliberations was finally announced on the 26th November 1959 - *Closure would not be objected to*. It is not known what objections may have been received from local sources, although it is reasonable to assume there were some.

WELFORD PARK by Charlie Marshall

Scenes at Welford Part in the 1950s by Charlie Marshall. At least two are taken from the high vantage points of the various signals. (The limited train service allowed plenty of time for other activities but it did mean that views of actual trains arriving or leaving were bound to be limited, for on these occasions there would be railway work to do.)

Top left - Viewed from the Down Inner Home Signal and with the exchange sidings devoid of traffic. Although the views are undated there are clues as to the actual time they were taken, which would appear to be around 1957/8. There is some suggestion that the munitions services witnessed a lull after 21st November 1957 and this could therefore be after this time. Clearly traffic was resumed later.

Top right - This view is slightly earlier, as witness the Down Main Staring Signal is still in the form of a wooden bracket - see illustration on page 84. The solitary van on the goods siding is vacuum fitted and may have arrived by passenger service.

Lower left - This time it is the vantage point of the Up Home Signal that affords the view. It is recalled that on one occasion a big end bearing failed on a steam engine approaching with a train from the direction of Boxford. The engine was declared a failure at Welford and placed in one of the sidings here until repairs could be affected.

Lower right - A down train has been signalled into the loop on this occasion. The lack of passengers meant there was rarely a need to object to using the platform for storage and what appear to be wagon tarpaulins are left on the platform. Behind are several new concrete fence posts, possibly left over from the construction of the military sidings.

WELFORD PARK by Charlie Marshall

Scenes from the south end of Welford Park, which was less frequently photographed.

Top left - Viewed from the Up Home Signal the throat of the military sidings is just visible on the left. Also on the left are the 'Sidings to Up Main Starting' and 'Sidings to Camp Line Starting' signals, both on the same post one above the other. This was slightly unusual as this type of junction signal, reading 'top to bottom left to right', had long since been superseded by the more conventional bracket type. Between the sidings and the running lines is an auxiliary token hut. This was provided so that a train arriving at the sidings could be quickly 'locked-in' thus freeing the running line. Likewise a train due to depart for Newbury could obtain a token as soon as the section to Newbury was clear without the need for a long walk by either the signalman or fireman. In practice limited traffic levels rendered this almost obsolete and it was rarely used.

Top right - Looking back from the camp line towards the station. The sand drag that protected the interchange sidings in the event of runaways is apparent. (See also colour illustration on page 116.)

Lower left - North towards the station and as before from the vantage point of a convenient signal post. In this view, clearly taken when the railway was still open to Lambourn, there has not been any traffic into or from the sidings for some time.

Lower right - The original and new bridges just south of the station. In the background are estate cottages.

WELFORD PARK by Charlie Marshall

From the vantage point of the signal seen in the centre view on this page, we can look back towards the station, the sand-drag being clearly visible. Whether this was ever needed in anger is not reported. In some respects the provision of what were in effect 'starting', and 'advance-starting' signals for what was in effect a private siding was slightly unusual, the siting of a 'home' was more easily explained as clearly this was a requirement to protect the BR sidings.

Almost the nearest we get to the camp itself, looking along the military line, the status of which as a private siding is signified by the gate in the distance. The two stop signals for the camp line, that seen here for trains from the camp and also that seen in the view on the top of the next page, were controlled by an open air ground frame of three levers, part of which is just visible (arrowed) on the extreme right hand corner of the view. This GF, electrically released from Welford Park signal box by lever No 10, also controlled the point for the sand-drag. Initially the GF had to be operated by the signalman, who would of course then leave the box for the purpose. Understandably this was not popular. Later the guard of the munitions train took charge. Officially Welford Park signal box should have been advised a train was due by means of a telephone call from the camp, although on occasions Charlie recalls a train might just 'appear' at the rear of the signal box. This would imply that formal working practices were not always adhered to. There was also a local telephone to the signal box located at the GF.

An LMS wagon label still in use for munitions from Stranraer Town. To Welford in 1957. The original was outlined with red lettering.

Almost the last rites at Lambourn. A photographer walks away from the single coach service, which has just arrived at the terminus. Staff outnumber passengers on this occasion. The various fixtures and fittings seen may be compared with the list on page 96. In the right background are what were known as Lock Meadow Cottages. These shook with the passing of the trains and which may well have contributed to one end collapsing shortly after the railway closed. They were subsequently demolished.

A cruel enlargement from the above view but depicting an essential, albeit rarely photographed item. This is the travelling safe used on a daily basis between Lambourn and Newbury. Intermediate stations on the branch would send their own takings daily to Lambourn in a leather cash bag which were then audited and assimilated into the main figures despatched to Newbury.

Meanwhile Paddington again appear to be hurrying, as just a week before someone, no name was given, had asked when a result might be expected. So why the hurry? We cannot be certain, but haste there certainly was, as closure notification was given for just six weeks after the TUCC decision, services between Newbury and Lambourn ending on Saturday 4th January 1960.

At this stage it might be enquired, why the haste? We simply do not know. Somewhere in the corridors of Paddington 'A.N. Other' had decreed the Lambourn line was to go. No serious attempt at economy, no attempt at attracting patronage. The branch to Lambourn would just be one of countless former GWR branch, secondary, cross-country and feeder routes deemed to be unnecessary in a forward looking rail network. It was anathema, an unnecessary drain on resources. Yet, in reality, without any form of up to date passenger census, how could Paddington be certain of how much the profit or loss was? Here we have to look again at the wider picture. Government, as always, was crying out for cuts in public expenditure. The railways were also trying at the same time to modernise. Money invested on new equipment meant that subsidies were not available. It was not the fault of the Western Region. The fault was higher up the tree, the railways were following the dictate of the politicians.

Closure came on a dark Saturday evening in January.

Lambourn goods shed seen from the yard side, with its small goods platform just visible. It is a great pity the dimensions and details of this structure were not recorded with the remainder of the inventory on pages 96/97. We shall never know what secrets were contained within.

Derek Clayton

DAVID ROSIER - Lad Porter at Lambourn: October 1956 to October 1959.

David Rosier left school in the summer of 1957, having for many years harboured the ambitions to be an engine driver. Unfortunately at the time, his eyesight was not considered sufficient and consequently the advice he received was to join the railway 'on the platform', "...promotion perhaps later meaning you might become a TTI (Travelling Ticket Inspector)....and at least be riding on trains". To David the latter was not ideal, but at least working on the railway was a start.

In the autumn of 1957, the shifts at Lambourn and likewise the duties of a Lad Porter, were in many respects similar to that described earlier - see page 31. Accordingly long periods were spent at Bockhampton Crossing, opening and closing the gates when necessary. With the gates closed across the road, David would wave a green flag to the driver to indicate all was clear, one driver in particular upon seeing this would wrench the regulator of his steam engine wide open causing David to step back somewhat sharpish. Even today David recalls that same man as being, "...a mad 'un".

When on late shift at the crossing and as soon as the last up train had passed, David should have walked back to the station to book off. The Lambourn line though was a friendly railway and it was the custom of the late turn signalman to do this for him, meaning he could instead walk the few yards from the crossing to his home in Bockhampton Lane, where he still lives today.

One night though, there was snow on the ground and whilst the last train from Newbury could be heard leaving Eastbury, the sound then became muffled and eventually died altogether. The next David knew was when a number of passengers walked past the crossing, the engine having become stuck in a snowdrift within the cutting beyond Eastbury station. The train was also unusually busy with passengers, many of whom were workers from the new atomic site at Harwell who had been forced to return by train, Didcot - Newbury -Lambourn, as the roads were impassable for their normal bus. The train crew did manage to dig it out themselves, but it was some time before the message came through by phone from the signalman for David to wait at his post. He recalls not finishing until nearer 11.00 pm that night. Normally this, the last train from Newbury ran to time, even though it was booked to wait for connections from a service arriving from Paddington and another from Weymouth. (Similar difficulties had occurred during the 1947 winter when the valley was virtually cut off apart from by rail).

On another occasion the first, empty, empty diesel car to arrive in the morning crashed through the gates, the driver having been travelling too fast in fog and misjudged his location. The baulks of timber were still on the front of the vehicle when it arrived at Lambourn. It took several weeks for a new set of gates to be provided, in the meanwhile four sheep hurdles were used as improvised gates, tied together across the roadway when necessary.

The shelter at Bockhampton was supplied with coal and kindling when required. David would fill a sack at the station and then ask the crew of the next train to drop it off as they passed.

At the station David recalls the usual round of cleaning, sweeping and polishing. "We would sweep the platform, it got very dirty, and then had to use a dustpan....watch out if Stan Knapp (Station Master) caught you sweeping it over the edge".

Like the Station Master, David was not keen on wearing his railway issue hat. (Stan wore a brown Trilby instead). But if the District Inspector, Mr Sullivan was on the way, out would come Stan Knapp's proper headgear. David would likewise be warned to put his hat on and also to, "...smarten yourself up lad...". He recalls it was not always easy to keep smart when climbing up and down from track level.

During the afternoon, one of the duties was to deliver the railway letters as well as any perishables which had arrived by the afternoon train, although these would have to be 'booked-in' first. Before setting out on his travels, David was invariably asked to fetch Mr Knapp his regular '20 Players', whilst Mr Knapps's wife 'Lotty', who was Clerk at the time, would invariably ask David to run an errand for her or perhaps even change her library book.

STATION GATES. LAMBOURN. X163.

David would likewise be given other jobs by the Station Master, perhaps to tidy the garden, located on the platform at the Newbury end of the building. When asked what Mr Knapp did all day, David's answer was quick and succinct, "...very little...'.

At this late stage there was still some racehorse traffic, but much traffic was also generated by the firm of Bushells, who would bring

Top - David Rosier (minus railway hat) posed by the gates at Bockhampton.

Right - David and Alan Marshall on the bridge over the River Lambourn a few yards north of Bockhampton Crossing. (Another view of this bridge will be found on page 35).

Opposite page - The station gates and approach road.

lorry loads of manure from the various stables and which was then shovelled by the lorry driver into open wagons. These were then sheeted and taken away. (Reg Hatter and Arthur Smith regularly came to Lambourn to assist in sheeting wagons when necessary). The contents would of course steam and had to be kept moist. In this way the wagons sometimes gave the impression they were on fire. At their destination the manure was treated to become mushroom compost. Lorries would also come into the yard to be weighed, the senior porter, 'Bunny' Brown doing most of the weighbridge work.

David recalls the goods shed being used to store traffic removed from railway wagons to avoid a demurrage payment having to be made. The goods shed was also where kindling, chopped sleepers, was kept, used for the office fires and as mentioned, for the hut fire at Bockhampton.

Another traffic, usually once a week, was a railway container containing rectangular tins of biscuits from Messrs. Scibbans-Kemp. (Despite extensive searching we are unable to afford much further information on this particular traffic). The railway container would be lifted off the wagon and gently lowered onto a waiting lorry by means of the yard crane. On one occasion the container was accidentally released before it had fully reached the lorry. No doubt broken biscuits inside.

David left the railway, he admits reluctantly, in October 1959. At the time he was concerned over being able to find a job following closure, but did venture out to witness the last train leaving Lambourn in January 1960. This departed accompanied by the sound of exploding detonators. (Stan Knapp he recalled, transferred to Hungerford after Lambourn closed.)

One of his regrets is not being to have a souvenir of the big lamp that was once on the gates at Bockhampton, "I really loved that lamp", he recounted.

Left - Horse box traffic appears to have been retained, from Lambourn at least, to the very end. The age of many of the vehicles in use also meant they would need the gas used for lighting replenished. Here vehicles await use at Lambourn.

Derek Clayton

Opposite - The public notice, dated as late as December 1959 advising of the withdrawal of services '"..on and from Monday 4th January 1960...". This particular board was at Speen.

Six coaches making up the last train which left Newbury with 59 passengers although this number had swelled to 126 by the time Lambourn was reached. Departure from Lambourn was also delayed as a result of the communication cord being pulled, 73 persons making that final poignant journey which eventually arrived back at Newbury 1 hour and 25 minutes late. Amongst those on board were two who had also travelled on the very first train 62 years earlier.

In the days immediately subsequent to the 4th January we do not know if here was ever a working north of Welford Park to collect wagons or other recoverable items. It is possible there actually was, for on 30th December a note in the file refers to Lambourn signal box closing, but to open again for clearance of yard traffic at Lambourn, East Garston and Great Shefford. What is known is that the GPO Telephone numbers, 'Lambourn 16' and 'Great Shefford 213' were disconnected shortly afterwards. In addition, the railway telephone circuit (No

524), and which had extensions in the Station Master's Office, Booking Office, and Signal Box at Lambourn, also at Bockhampton Crossing, at East Garston and Great Shefford was similarly taken out of use. The railway telephones at Boxford and Speen were retained, (There was never a telephone at Stockcross), although both were moved slightly. At Boxford, to the Ground Frame at the north end of the site and at Speen to a point nearer to the level crossing.

At Welford Park, so far as goods traffic was concerned, it was business as usual. A thrice weekly freight was booked to run on Monday, Wednesday and Friday, departing from Newbury at 12.10 pm and returning from Welford at 1.30 pm. Welford Park itself was advised as open for business from 8.00 am to 5.00 pm on weekdays and 8.00 am to 12.00 pm on Saturdays. Contemporary correspondence refers to a sign affording these details being provided at the station entrance, but it is not clear if this was in fact, provided.

What is probably a horse box special being shunted at Newbury, whilst the branch railcar waits in the bay. For years there was a sign on the down platform at Newbury which, according to George Behrend, "... must have been rusted in position....". It proclaimed, 'Over the bridge for the Lambourn Train,' again according to Behrend, "...regardless of the time of day or whether a Lambourn train might possibly be present."

Derek Clayton

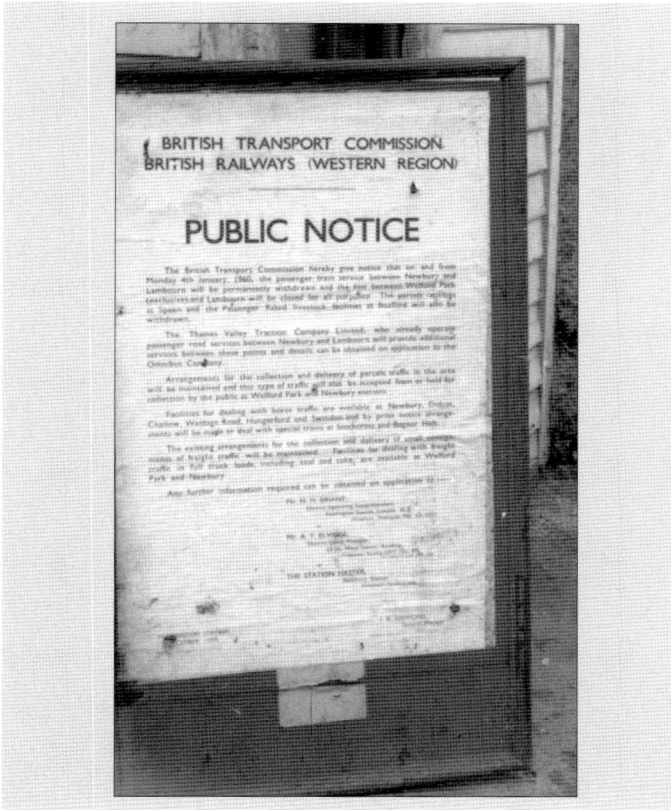

The signal box also remained operational between 9.15 am and 4 35 pm on weekdays, meaning there was still conventional token working from Newbury West. It is not known if any signalling items, notably the token machines for the section north to Lambourn, were recovered, or if these were left for scrap, the former being more likely.

In addition to the booked goods workings, there were still special workings of munitions to and from the sidings. It was probably for this reason that it was decided to retain the signal box as a block post. Staffing was now by a reliefman from Newbury, although on the days when the regular goods working did not run and there was no munitions traffic, it was, no doubt, a quiet posting..

Despite the urgency in affecting closure, there was no immediate rush to dismantle the track nor sell the land.

Under the canopy at Lambourn and with the position of the station clock also shown. Left to right the doors are marked, 'Station Master', 'Private' (This was the Booking Office, but was accessed from the waiting room). 'Waiting Room' and 'Ladies Room'. The station was built on sloping ground which meant at the rear there were supporting arches, with access to all the facilities only from the platform side. A second clock was located in the Waiting Room. The origins of this item, which still survive in the Lambourn archives, are unknown. Whilst similar to, it is by no means certain to have originated from the GWR and does not display an 'ivorine' identification number.

Colin Martin / The Transport Treasury

Indeed in a Paddington memorandum of the 2nd December 1959, J.R. Hammond, in the General Manager's office, stated that facilities north of Welford were to remain in situ for nine months after closure. The same memorandum also noted that the remaining freight services to Welford would be operated on the 'One engine in steam' principal. This did not occur until 3rd July 1962, when Welford Park signal box was officially closed and the line then became, in effect, a long siding controlled by a wooden train staff. When not in use this item was retained in Newbury West signal box.

As part of the supposed concentration of railhead facilities for general goods at Welford Park, it was agreed that the Loading Gauge from Lambourn would be transferred to Welford. An official record of the 7th December 1959 comments that this item is to be transferred from Welford Park to Lambourn! Someone at Paddington transposed the names. The previous note about the weighbridge and building being moved from Lambourn was now stated not to be taking place, as the expense involved could not be justified.

Meanwhile, at Welford Park, the signal box now also doubled as goods office and checkers office. Two coal merchants, Messrs Bodman at Lambourn and Bates at East Garston retained their sites at what were now closed stations, at the same time receiving supplies by rail as far as Welford. Later the names G Bodman and F Green are referred to, both seemingly from Lambourn.

Although making perhaps somewhat depressing reading, on the 28th January Paddington compiled a detailed list of all assets to be disposed of. This consisted "The whole of the track beyond the temporary stop-blocks now erected at Welford Park, 6m 40ch., including the sidings at Great Shefford, East Garston and Lambourn. Also the branch bay and loop lines at Newbury and connection at the Welford Park end at Boxford." The former Lambourn bay line at Newbury would, in fact, remain in situ for some time whilst mention of the connection at the north end of Boxford loop meant the earlier reference to repositioning the telephone to the ground frame at this location would be irrelevant.

The list itself, which is included overleaf, is in full of interest, containing much detail of the actual stations. It

Buildings, Structures, etc (Passenger and Parcels)	
LAMBOURN	<u>Station entrance.</u> Common entrance to passenger station and goods yard by way of a gate 15' 6" wide from Station Road. There is also a footpath 6' 3" wide and a 5' fence 9' 9" wide making the overall width of BTC property on approach road 31' 6". The distance from the station gate to the middle of the slope to the platform is 75'.
	<u>Platform.</u> Including approach slopes 355' 7" in length. Gate at beginning of platform ramp 18' 4", plus pavement 5' 7" making the total width of the approach slope 23' 11". Width of platform proper 12' 4". Wooden fence for the whole length of the platform proper, except where buildings intervene. 6 electric lamps on platform and approach.
	<u>Office Block.</u> Brick built 59' 8" x 13' 5". Covered by veranda extending for the whole length of the building and projecting to platform edge a further 12 ' 4". The office block comprises:-
	<u>Station Master's Office.</u> 12' 6" x 8' 3" with glass door light above 2' 8" x 1' 3". Door to booking office (wooden) 6' 6" x 2' 3". 3 windows 5' 6" x 2' 4", 1 fixed cupboard 9' x 3', 1 Courtier Stove No 3F, 1 fixed shelf 4' x 6', 1 fixed shelf 3' 3" x 1', 1 wash basin. 2 electric lamps.
	<u>Booking Office.</u> 12' 6" x 10' 7" with door to platform (wooden) 7' 6" x 3' with glass door light above 2' 8" x 1' 3". 3 windows 5' 6" x 2'4 ", 1 fixed shelf 11' 6" x 1' 3", 1 fixed shelf 3' 3" x 1' 3", I fixed shelf 3' x 1' 9", 3 fixed shelves 3' x 1' 6". 1 book rack 3' 5" x 1' 6" x 11", 1 nest pigeon holes 3' 4" x 3' 10", 1 counter 11' 5" x 3' 3" x 2' 4" with 2 cupboards, I bookrack and 9 drawers. 1 Osbrite stove, 2 electric lamps.
	<u>Waiting Room.</u> 12' 6" x 14' 11" with door to platform (wooden) 7' 3" x 3' 4" with glass door light above 2' 8" x 1' 3". 5 windows 5' 6" x 2' 4". I fireplace with fender. 1 crush barrier (metal and wood) 3' x 3', 1 booking window 1' 5" x 1' 9", 1 electric lamp.
	<u>Ladies Rooms.</u> Waiting room 12' 6" x 10' 5", with entrance 3'3" x 3' 9". Toilet 5' 9" x 3' 4" with vestibule 4' 3" x 3' 4". Door to platform (wood and frosted glass) 7' 3" x 3'. Door to Ladies Waiting Room (wooden) 6'9 " x 2' 5". Door to toilet vestibule (wooden) 6' 6" x 2' 5", door to toilet (wood and frosted glass) 6' 6" x 2' 5". 3 windows 5' 6" x 2' 4". 1 fireplace with fender. 7 fixed shelves 3' x 1' 4". 3 electric lights. Window in toilet vestibule 2' 3" x 5' 6", 1 toilet with cistern and pan, window in toilet 2' 3" x 2' 6".
	<u>Gent's Lavatory.</u> 12' 6" x 6' 1" with door to platform (wooden) 7' 2" x 3', wooden screen around door 5' 6" x 9' 2" x 6' 6", door to toilet (wood and frosted glass) 6' 4" x 2' 4", 2 windows (frosted glass) 2' 3" x 2', 3 stalls with 1 cistern, 1 toilet with cistern and pen, 1 cold water tap, 1 electric lamp.
	<u>Other Buildings on Platform.</u> Parcels Office (corrugated iron) 13' 3" x 9' 6" with door 7' 3". 1 window 3' 8" x 2' 9", 1 window 3' x 4', 1 Courtier stove No 3F, 1 luggage rack 5' 10" x 2' 9" x 6' 6", 1 counter 6' 5" x 2' 6" x 3' 3" sloping to 2' 8" with 2 drawers and 1 cupboard. 1 boot rack. Store Shed (corrugated iron) 20' x 7' with double doors 6' 6" x 4'.
	<u>Other Buildings and Structures.</u> Oil hut (corrugated iron) 8' x 6' 2". Signal Box (wooden) 17' 1" x 10'. Carriage Cleaners Hut (metal) 4' 6" x 6' 6". Water Tower No 1. Coal pen (wooden) Horse Loading Dock 278' x 22' 9" with 1 concrete lamp hoist. Station House - when vacated by present Station Master. (The exact location of the station house was not given.)
	<u>Station Signs etc.</u> 'Lambourn' 10' 5" x 2' on iron posts 7' high. 'Waiting Room' double sign 4' x 1' and 4' x 1', 'Ladies Room' double sign 4' x 1' and 4' x 1', 'Ladies Room' 1' 8" x 5'. 'Gentleman' double sign 4' x 1' and 4' x 1'. 'Gentleman 1' 6" x 3½" 'Station Master' 2' x 3½", 'Private' 1' 6" x 3½", 'Booking Office' 2'x 3½", 'Tickets' 1' 5" x 2½', 'Please adjust your dress' 1' 3" x 9".

Note - there is no reference whatsoever to the wooden goods shed at Lambourn. Instead it was noted that "Details of buildings etc. in goods yard will be supplied by the Goods Commercial Manager".

In a separate but related document, dated 5th July 1960, the Chief Mechanical Engineer's Department gave details of the fixed assets at Lambourn for which they were responsible. These were the 3,000 gallon pillar tank, its associated water supply piping and valves, and a 3-ton fixed hand crane, No FM2687. The original cost of the first item, dating from 1910, was put at £160, whilst at 1960 prices the cost of recovery was £155 against a scrap value of just £60. Some of the associated pipework, presumably lead, was evidently thought uneconomic to recover, even though its replacement cost in 1960 was put at £190. The yard crane dating from 1929, originally cost £158 and was worth £44 in scrap. It could be removed for just £5. Whether any or all of these items were in fact subsequently recovered by the railway or left for the scrap merchant is not known.

BOCKHAMPTON CROSSING	Crossing Keeper's hut with door 6' x 2". 2 windows 1' 3" x 1' 3". 1 oil hut (corrugated iron) 3' 6" x 2' 7 " x 7'. 2 warning lamps (oil). 1 notice 'Trespassers' 2' 1' on post 5' high.
EASTBURY	Platform 198' 6" x 10' with wire fence on wooden posts 5' high whole length of platform. 4 wooden lamp posts 2 with lamps. 1 wooden shelter with iron roof 10' 10" x 6' 4" with door 7' 3" x 3', fixed wooden seat on 3 sides. 1 entrance gate 5' 8" x 5' 3", 1 concrete lamp hoist. Station sign 'Eastbury' 8' 4" x 1' 10" on iron posts 6' 10" high.
EAST GARSTON	Platform 19' 8" x 108' 6" with wire fence on concrete posts 4' 6" high for whole length of platform except where shelter and loading gates intervene. Office (wooden) 9' 7" x 5' 5" with door (wood with glass panels) 6' x 2' 2". 1 window clear and frosted glass 1' 3" x 2' 2". 1 window 1' 9" x 2' 5". 1 booking window 1' 6" x 1' 8". 1 counter 5' 5" x 1' 9" x 3' 3" with cupboard, drawer and shelf. I fixed wooden seat 7' 6" x 1' 2". 1 entrance gate 5' 7" x 5' 3". Station sign 'East Garston' 11' 7" on iron posts 7' high. 1 notice 'Trespassers' 2' x 1'. 2 posts with lamps. 1 concrete lamp hoist. Double gate in platform forming lorry loading dock 7' 2" x 4' 6". 1 warning lamp (oil) at crossing. 1 corrugated iron shelter 20' x 7' with fixed wooden seat on 3 sides, double doors 4' 6" x 6' 3", 2 windows 2' 3" x 2' 3", 1 oil lamp.
GREAT SHEFFORD	Platform 189' x 10' 6" with wire fence on wooden posts 4' 6" high whole length of platform. Office (wooden) 10' 8" x 7' 4" with double door (wood and glass) 4' 10" x 6' 8" including booking window. 2 windows 2' 10" x 3' 6". Desk with cupboard 1' 11" x 3' 8". 1 counter 3' 3" x 3' 6" x 9' with shelf. 1 fixed wooden seat 5' x 1' 3". 1 Tortoise stove. 2 fixed shelves 1' 9" x 9" x 5". Station sign 'Great Shefford' 13' 4" x 2' on iron posts 6' 6" high. 1 corrugated iron shelter 20' x 7' with fixed wooden seat on 3 sides. Double doors 4' 7" x 6' 2", 2 windows 2' 2" x 2' 2". 1 concrete lamp hoist, 1 iron lamp holder, 1 double entrance gate 4' 6" x 6'.
WELFORD PARK	Up platform 205' 7" x 10' 4" with wire fence on concrete posts whole length of platform. 1 metal lamp post, 1 concrete lamp hoist. 2 corrugated iron shelters 20' x 7' with fixed wooden seat on 3 sides. Double doors 4' 10" x 6' 3", 2 windows in each shelter 2' 3" x 2' 3". 2 station signs ' Welford Park' each 12' 4" on iron posts 6' 2" high. (*The wooden ticket office was not included and presumably then was considered to be required.*)
BOXFORD	Platform 198' x 12' 2". Office (wooden) 10' 7" x 7' 8" with double door 6' 10" x 4' 10", 2 windows 2' 9" x 3' 6". 1 fixed desk with cupboard 2' 3" x 2' 3" x 3' 6". 1 counter 3' 1" x 1' 6" x 9' with drawer and shelf. 1 Tortoise stove. 1 fixed bench-type seat 3' 5" x 1' 3" 1 corrugated iron shelter 20' x 7' with fixed wooden seat on 3 sides. Double doors 6' 2" x 4' 7", 2 windows 2' 3" x 2' 3". Station sign 'Boxford' 7' 10" x 2' on iron posts 6' 4" high. 3 iron lamp-posts, 1 concrete lamp hoist, 1 Elsan.
STOCKCROSS and BAGNOR	1 corrugated iron shelter 20' x 7' with fixed wooden seat on 3 sides. Double doors 6' 2" x 4' 8", 2 windows 2' 3" x 2' 3". 1 Station sign 'Stockcross and Bagnor' 11' 5" x 2' 7" on iron posts 7' 10" high.
SPEEN	Platform 201' x 12' 1 corrugated iron shelter 20' x 7' with fixed wooden seat on 3 sides. Double doors 6' 2" x 4' 8", 2 windows 2' 3" x 2' 3". 1 bench type platform seat (fixed) 8'. 1 Station sign 'Speen' 6' 5" x 1' 10" on iron posts 7' 5" high. 1 Elsan. 1 concrete lamp hoist. 3 iron lamp posts. Office (wooden) 6' x 10' 4" with door 6' 2" x 2' 8".1 counter 3' 4" x 4' 6" x 2' with shelf, drawer and cupboard. 1 stove (make unknown)..

shows what has been believed of the former GWR, that whilst everything might appear to be standard, if the various dimensions are to be believed then 'standardisation' in practice very different. Of course, it may also be that whoever did the measuring was not absolutely accurate. This may well be the case, as items such as the corrugated iron 'Pagoda' type huts should indeed have been to a uniform type.

But, with the line closed, was there really much point in sending staff out to record the scene in such detail? No doubt these persons, and there would have been two,

travelled by road. They could not have reached the closed stations otherwise, but we may well question whether it was all worthwhile.

Other items, furniture, ticket stocks would have been recovered quickly, whilst a note in the paperwork for the 26th January refers to 'time pieces' being recovered and sent to the Signal Engineer at Reading.

Nothing much seems to have taken place for the next few months, although, on the 23rd May 1960, a note from R G Henbest at the Estates and Rating Department, states he has been approached by one of the neighbouring

property owners, who wished to purchase the whole of the materials between Welford and Lambourn. The question of sale would rumble on for several months, not helped by the fact that, of the materials north of Welford, 440 tons of rail was considered serviceable and a further 1,145 tons was of scrap value, together with 9½ tons of girders. There were also some 8,000 cubic yards of ballast. At some stage in the proceedings the figure of £16,000 is quoted as offered by the un-named prospective purchaser.

Meanwhile, so far as the remaining, operational, section of the railway was concerned, the subject of 'Stop' boards and sighting distances at Speen level crossing come under discussion. In July 1960, seven months after closure, stop boards had still not been provided, despite having been approved in December of the previous year. The working timetables show that freight trains were allowed five minutes for opening and closing the crossing gates at Speen. Marker boards were eventually approved sometime after May 1962.

Whilst negotiations on the disposal of assets may have been proceeding slowly, Paddington were also keen to effect further asset stripping on what was left south of Welford. This comes in the form of a memorandum, dated the 11th August 1960, which gives an estimated cost of £850 for alterations to be carried out at Welford Park, Boxford, and Speen together with £220 for the removal of the Lambourn bay and sidings at Newbury. At Welford the work was to demolish the former up platform, waiting room and shed and to provide two stop boards. At Boxford, again the platform and buildings would be demolished as well as taking up a single connection. At Speen the task was to demolish the platform and buildings and provide 3(?) stop boards. Thus the task of recording in such finite detail the facilities at these locations had proved futile. In reality, whilst the task may have been to ascertain if anything might have a use elsewhere, what little was eventually salvaged for re-use was really obvious from the outset.

What may well have been an expected move now came, in a hand-written note where it was stated that most of the usable signalling equipment would in fact be recovered. This was stated to be, at Lambourn, the signal box and signals, the south and north ground frames at East Garston and Great Shefford, at Welford Park the signal box to be stripped, all signalling equipment removed and the box to be used as a

Top - Lambourn in its final days. No more will passengers surmount the ramp to gain access to the platform, offices and trains. No more will the offices be swept, the lamps lit, the parcels carried. A way of life would end on a dark January Saturday in early 1960. Paddington was carrying out the edict of the higher echelons of British Railways and in turn were following government dictat.

Derek Clayton

Bottom - A Daily Account sheet used at the staffed intermediate stations on the line and as was sent to Lambourn daily.

checkers cabin. Control of the various turnouts at Welford formerly worked from the signal box would now be by 2-lever ground frames. At Boxford both ground frames would be recovered, whilst at Speen the level crossing gates would be padlocked across the railway, the key being carried on the Train Staff. Finally some locking alterations were envisaged at Newbury West. It would appear as if freight traffic was to finally cease at Boxford, for with no siding there would be nowhere to leave a vehicle. However, the Freight Working Timetables for both 1961 and 1962 still show the timetabled train(s) having a five minute wait in the up direction. It may therefore be open to debate as to when the recovery of assets at the intermediate stations between Welford and Newbury was actually carried out, possibly at the time Welford Park signal box was finally closed in July 1962. It is known that whilst BR may well have recovered various items of signalling equipment north of Welford, (although it is cannot be confirmed if they actually did), the structure of Lambourn signal box itself was left in situ.

We now need to revert to the undertaking given by BR to the TUCC at the time of closure, that the line would remain in situ, albeit moribund, for nine months following closure. In itself this is, perhaps, slightly strange. Did BR, in their haste, to close the line realise that might well be a later challenge?

There is no evidence to support this, save a note from C W Powell at Paddington to another Paddington official dated the 1st January 1960, in which he states, "...it has been agreed with the South Eastern TUCC the facilities between Welford Park and Lambourn remain for nine months after discontinuance of the services. Therefore no steps can be taken for the recovery of redundant assets on this section of line until this period has expired." It must be said that nowhere in the correspondence bundle is there reference to anything like a change of heart, or consideration to restore services.

Almost a year had passed since closure, when it was mentioned on 30th December 1960 that the redundant materials between Welford Park and Lambourn had been sold to a Mr R A Denton for £19,000. Evidently, despite the railway's best intentions at salvage what was considered re-useable signalling material, this had not taken place by February 1961, for two notes appear in the paperwork at this time. The first was that Paddington might well try and persuade the Air Ministry to contribute towards the simplification of the signalling as far as Welford, on the basis that this will be of benefit to the military in reducing their own contribution towards maintenance. This is a strange remark to make and implies that an agreement was

Stockcross and Bagnor some years after closure. Despite the effort made by the Western Region to record and potentially salvage reusable items, the only thing to have been removed would appear to be the station nameboard.

Lambourn, Autumn 1961. At this time and indeed for a further two years, George Bodman would continue to retain his coal yard at the station site although of course now receiving supplies at Welford Park. On 28th November 1963 he was given notice to quit the station, from which time his coal yard was located at his home. Following withdrawal of freight facilities (aside from Air Ministry traffic) at Welford, coal would arrive by rail at Hungerford. This arrangement continued until May 1968 when that station too ceased to retain facilities for receiving coal. From then on coal would arrive at Lambourn by road. Located behind the photographer was the weighbridge hut, which appears also to have generally escaped the camera.

Pat Legg Collection

Eastbury (Halt) devoid of track. The wooden shelter was a real relic. Had it been identified as such it was the last survivor of the original Lambourn Valley Railway wooden shelters dating from 1898, all the others having been replaced some years earlier. It deserved a better fate than to be left to the vandals or scavengers. By 1929 all the stopping places on the line, with the exception of Lambourn, were also formerly classified as 'Halts', even though this designation was not always displayed in practice.

already in place between the railways and military. Clearly something must have been arranged some years earlier, although, as will be referred to later, some aspects of operating the line for military traffic were never enshrined in agreement form throughout its existence, afterwards a draft agreement for operation of the Private Siding at Welford is referred to on the 24th April 1961, some seven years after the Welford facility was first brought into use. It was never signed by the Ministry. Additionally, the WR Signal department remarked that 'due to other heavy (unspecified) commitments', they were unable to undertake removal of the recoverable assets themselves.

Mr Denton in the meanwhile had made it known that his principal interest was in the sleepers and it appears he asked if the railway would remove any rail they themselves might wish to salvage. Again the resources question was raised. Paddington it seemed unable to accede to the request, this time due to an acute staff shortage.

With Welford Park now a simple goods facility, it was suddenly realised that there were no catch point in place, to prevent stock that might be stabled in the former down platform running back towards Newbury. That in the Newbury direction there was a rising gradient of 1 in 120 for a short distance was evidently considered an insufficient barrier. Consequently, a local instruction was issued that no stock was to be stabled in the former down platform.

Meanwhile, despite the apparent sale of assets, these were evidently still in situ and no action could for the present be taken on a request to purchase the former railway trackbed fronting Eastbury Manor. The interested party was E M Baylis & Co.

Shortly afterwards matters appeared to be moving towards the final removal of the track north of Welford, although not before on the 21st July 1961, the Station Master at Newbury, Mr Cox, received an unexpected letter

from Messrs Pitrail Ltd of Aldridge, Staffordshire who advised Mr Cox that they had two wagons, Nos. M611229 and M613676, waiting at Newbury and ready to worked to Welford Park in readiness for 'uplifting the track'.

At Newbury Mr Cox was evidently unsure what to do. Paddington, it appears had been acting without advising him of progress. This included selling off the land of the former railway to just two local farmers, He was thus the brunt of complaints from landowners, who assured the local press that they had, in turn, been assured by the BTC that would themselves receive first refusal for land adjoining their properties.

Newbury therefore sought advice from Paddington, 'soonest', especially as Pittrail referred to collecting the wagons from Welford with their own locomotive. Paddington, not un-naturally, wanted to know in return where this locomotive might be placed on the rails. Pittrial had also asked about working redundant assets to Reading Goods, although enquiries here revealed Reading had apparently lost that record of correspondence.

Mr Cox at Newbury was adamant, that until he received authority from Paddington, he would not allow the Pittrail wagons to pass beyond the stop-blocks at Welford Park. (The original letter from Pittrail was addressed to the '...The Station Master' Welford Park...'.)

Paddington, it seems, were also in the dark, but they did move fast, not only now writing to Pittrail to enquire about that company's intentions, but it also appears that someone at Swindon had been made aware that anything considered worthy of salvage should be removed forthwith.

There were two results. The first was from Swindon stores department, on the 26th July, which referred to a 5cwt portable weighbridge from Great Shefford, not mentioned on the inventory, which had been lost in transit and also the original 20T cart weighbridge from Lambourn might be used at Gloucester Eastgate Goods. The weighbridge was indeed removed by road lorry from Lambourn to Swindon and may presumably have finished its days as suggested. Ironically, it would also appear this was possibly the only item of hardware north of Welford that did find further use.

Five days later, Messrs Pittrail responded to Paddington, stating that their own locomotive would be arriving at Lambourn by road although they would require a number of bogie bolster wagons. The eventual number is thought to have been 52 wagons, to be delivered to Welford Park. At the same time it became clear to Paddington that, unbeknown to the railway, Messrs Pittrail had been employed by Mr Denton and that, as contractors, they wished to begin work on the 14th August.

This, however, was slightly premature as it was not until the 30th August that Paddington confirmed that a cheque for payment had been received from Mr Denton and that the removal of assets might now take place.

From this point on we can only surmise on the activity north of Newbury. The Pittrail locomotive, a Ruston Diesel, had evidently arrived at Lambourn a few days earlier and work then progressed on track removal. The contractors used the goods loops at East Garston and Great Shefford for running round, whilst it was agreed that, when this was deemed necessary at Welford Park, the signalman there would withdraw a token for the section to

Military traffic approaching Welford from the camp. BR wagons were used, although within the camp there it is believed there were several 'internal user' vehicles. Seen is No 9011, one of a pair of 0-4-0 Diesel Mechanical shunters, built by Ruston Hornsby in 1956. This and an identical sister locomotive, No 9012 were sent new to the site in 1956. (Locomotive details prior to this date are not known.) After 1970 a number of other standard MoD diesel locomotives were used, including at least one standard Army 350hp shunter, No 601, as late as 1973. This particular locomotive subsequently went to Bicester. Following the closure of the line at Welford, 9011 and 9012 were sent to the nearby Thatcham depot.

Possibly the same train and occasion as seen on the previous page although at a slightly differing location. BR paperwork appertaining to the line from Welford variously describes the route as 'Air Ministry', 'Ministry of Defence', 'USAAF', 'Camp Line' etc. Officially it was under the control of the Air Ministry until 1ˢᵗ April 1964 after which time it became the Ministry of Defence, Air Force Department, Welford Park. The engines carried a blue livery.

Newbury and hold it out of the machine until the manoeuvre had taken place. The way in which Pittrail operated still seem strange today, delivering wagon loads of rails to Welford, but then still seemingly able to return their locomotive to Lambourn for eventual recovery by road…..?

Similarly we do not know how long the work of dismantling took although we do know that the line was severed at Welford around early October. There are no photographs of the work and no BR record. The latter was hardly surprising, as the railway was no longer involved. All else that is known is hearsay, a local farmer, evidently thinking he would pick up a bargain, agreed to purchase a considerable number of sleepers from the line, whether this was from the contractor is not known. His purchase though, yielded not what he had expected, which was wooden sleepers, but the concrete variant. The use for these as

salvage was nil. It would appear also that north of Welford the land was eventually dissected and sold to the owners of adjoining property. By whom, to whom, and at what price, is beyond the remit of this work.

It might be tempting to hope that after all the various actions and inactions over the closure and sale of the line north of Welford, that from this time onwards a more organised regime would emerge. After all the line was now simply a long siding, stop blocks having been re-established at 6m 39½ch, presumably the same point as before, just north of Welford. The issue of the stop-blocks would rumble on for some time. One department stated that these could be replaced, another stating that they had no authority to do so, and that only temporary ones would be provided.

Despiite much correspondence to the contrary, it

appears the signal department had still not found the time to convert the truncated line from its original electric token operation to that of one engine in steam. This was also proving to be costly, as, on the 15th September 1961, a note from Mr Cox at Newbury, stated that each time a train was required to run to Welford, a relief signalman must be sent, which involved 4 hours overtime payment. Newbury stated, "As I often have to arrange additional trips to cover requirements of ammunition trains ex USAF at Welford I estimate we are spending £12 per week in overtime (£600 p.a.) unnecessarily." The suggestion was made, as a temporary measure, to permanently withdraw a token, spike or clip all points and use a pilotman.

Possibly spurred by the realisation that inaction over an obvious economy was costing money, on the 17th November 1961 there was, at last, a formal proposal for the simplification of the signalling, as per the plans on the next 4 pages.

Throughout this time munitions traffic was passing over the line, both to and from Welford. This is confirmed in a letter dated the 19th December 1961, in which it was stated that it was sometimes necessary for the Western Region to hire an engine for traffic to what was by then, the USAF at Welford. This had taken place on Sunday 19th November, and also two days later. In both cases this was to prepare loads for subsequent shipping to Felixstowe and Milford Haven.

Indeed, some detail is available of the first day, when the BR locomotive made six trips from Welford Park to the base and moved 102 loaded and 49 empty vehicles. The corresponding figures were 101 and 24 on the Tuesday. The maximum load taken down the incline was 27 loaded wagons. On the Sunday, the final train was formed of 15 loaded and 8 barrier wagons, which then proceeded to Newbury. Presumably balance of 87 loaded wagons was left in sidings at Welford Park station?

At this stage there was no mention of exactly what the railway motive power was, although a few weeks later it was confirmed as having been a steam locomotive of the 22xx type. This engine was provided by Reading shed, although the driver from Reading would change footplates with the driver of the Newbury diesel pilot, as only he had route knowledge to Welford. It was thus necessary that the Reading man also be diesel competent.

Locomotives of the 22xx type were used as no water was available at Welford which would have prohibited use of a 57xx. For operational reasons, train weights proceeding up the 1 in 80 gradient from Welford Park to the base were also restricted to 15 wagons. This was so that the engine would be able to restart on the gradient should the gates at the base not be open.

Although this type of hiring and operation had been going on for some time, a suggestion was made that a test should be carried out to assess suitability. The fact that a successful operation had already been carried out was evidently of little consequence. There is a note that a 350hp diesel shunter may also have been hired by BR to the USAF around this time. This cannot be confirmed.

The signalling alterations eventually became a reality in July 1962. The former 'B' pattern Electric token was replaced by a wooden train staff, also of 'B' pattern', labelled 'Newbury West - Welford Park'. This incorporated an Annett's key, to unlock the Boxford ground frame. A recovered catch point from Newbury was also placed on the single line at Newbury, where the former Lambourn bay was scheduled to be removed about the same time. The Lambourn bay, at the west end of Newbury station, had survived partly because of appalling inaction by the Western Region in the past two years. Ironically this was to the railways advantage, as at this time was the rebuilding of the Newbury by-pass bridge at the east end of the station site. In connection with this work the Reading / Didcot bay, also used for parcels traffic, was inaccessible for some time, meaning the former Lambourn Bay would see its final use for parcels traffic. It survived in this way until at least the end of 1963.

Actual conversion of the line from ETT to OES took place, as mentioned, on the 3rd July. On this date new stop boards were provided at Speen, to indicate the position past the crossing at which it was necessary to wait, according to the length of the train behind. These signified 10, 20, or, the maximum for the branch, 30 wagon trains. Boards were also provided at Welford and on the approach to Newbury. The 1962 note relating to this, whilst written on BR headed paper was stamped 'GWR District Inspectors Office Newbury' Clearly the DI, Mr R (Bob) J Sullivan believed in maintaining tradition.

With in future no bay line to act as a diversion for trains coming off the branch, it was a requisite that some form of safety be provided, to protect the main line. Hence the inclusion of the previously mentioned catch point. It is worth mentioning that at various times there had been suggestions for a revised connection between the branch and the main lines, slightly west of Newbury. The purpose of this was to allow a re-alignment of the main lines for faster running in the vicinity of the road bridge at the immediate end of the station. This was something that did take place in later years, although by that time the Lambourn branch was but a memory.

Returning to 1962, in June it was reported that the new 'one engine in steam' operation could cause operational difficulties, should the USAF request a BR locomotive to shunt at Welford when a BR freight was already at Welford. Under these circumstances the train would have to return to Newbury before a locomotive could be sent out. It would either have had to be 'locked-in' at Welford and the staff returned by road, or have completed its shunt and returned, before the line could again be released for ordinary BR traffic. BR's concern over the reliability of the USAF diesel shunters was unwarranted, as it was mentioned that there had only been two failures in the past five years,. The occasions being the 19th and 20th November 1961 which were referred to previously. Later, in September 1962, someone realised that the 350 hp diesel

WELFORD PARK Nº 2 GF

Nº   RELEASED BY

② ANNETTS KEY 'A' FROM
~~K.R.I. Nº1GF~~ CHECKER'S CABIN

DEPOT

TO BE
SPIKED CLI...
PADLOCKE...
OF USE.

SB TO BE RETAINED
AS CHECKER'S CABIN

OM LAMBOURN

②

△ 2

△ 1

II

△ 1

II

B

STOP BOARD WITH TELEPHONE
TO CHECKERS CABIN TO BE
PROVIDED

BOXFORD
2 LEVER

II

STOP BLOCK TO BE PROVIDED

CATCHPOINT TO BE SPIKED
CLIPPED & PADLOCKED
OUT OF USE

WELFORD PARK Nº 1 GF   TO BE PROVIDED

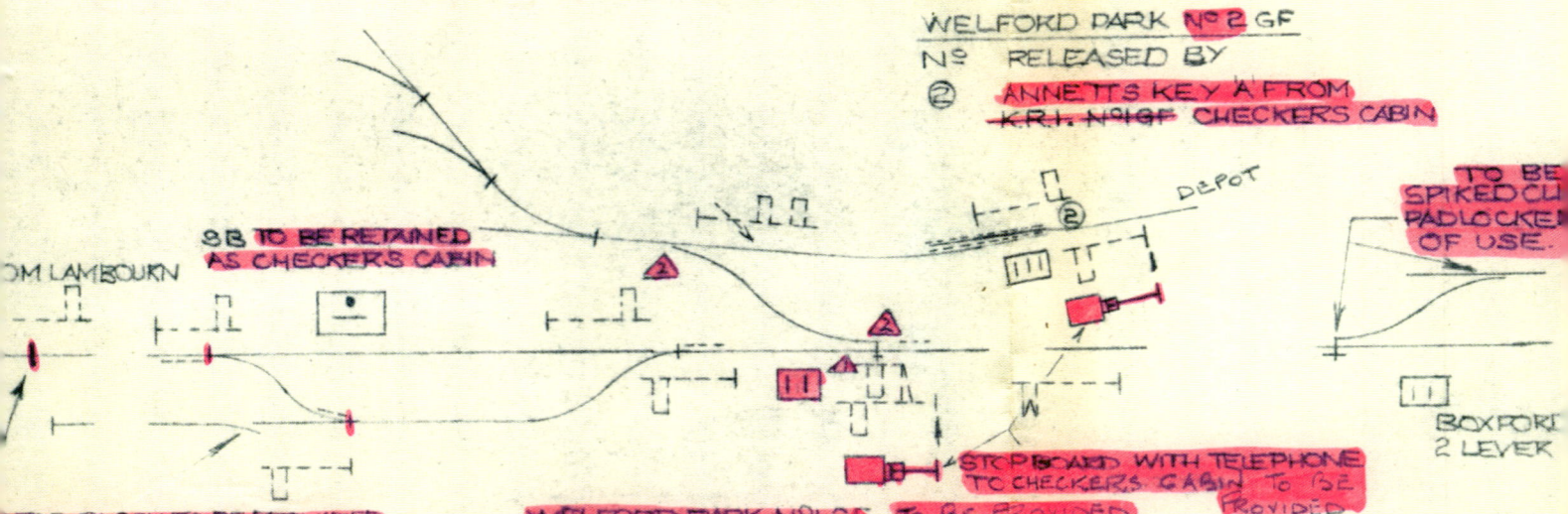

Nº	RELEASED BY	RELEASES
△ 1	'B' PATT : ANNETTS KEY ON WOODEN TRAIN STAFF	△ 2
△ 2	△ 1 AND ANNETTS KEY 'A' FROM CHECKER'S CABIN	

WELFORD PARK S.B
23 LEVER W.R. H.T 4" CENTRES
ALL SIGNALLING EQUIPMENT TO
BE RECOVERED

LOCAL C

THE UNDERSIGNED,
PURPOSES AND GEN
IT SHOULD

Officer

DISTRICT ENGINEER

DISTRICT COMMERCIAL MAN

DISTRICT OPERATING

DISTRICT MOTIVE POWER SUP

AREA WELFARE OF

STATION MASTER

GOODS AGENT

AMENDMENTS

NEWB

PROPOS...

Proposals for the implantation of 'One Engine in Steam' working between Newbury and Welford Park, November 1961.

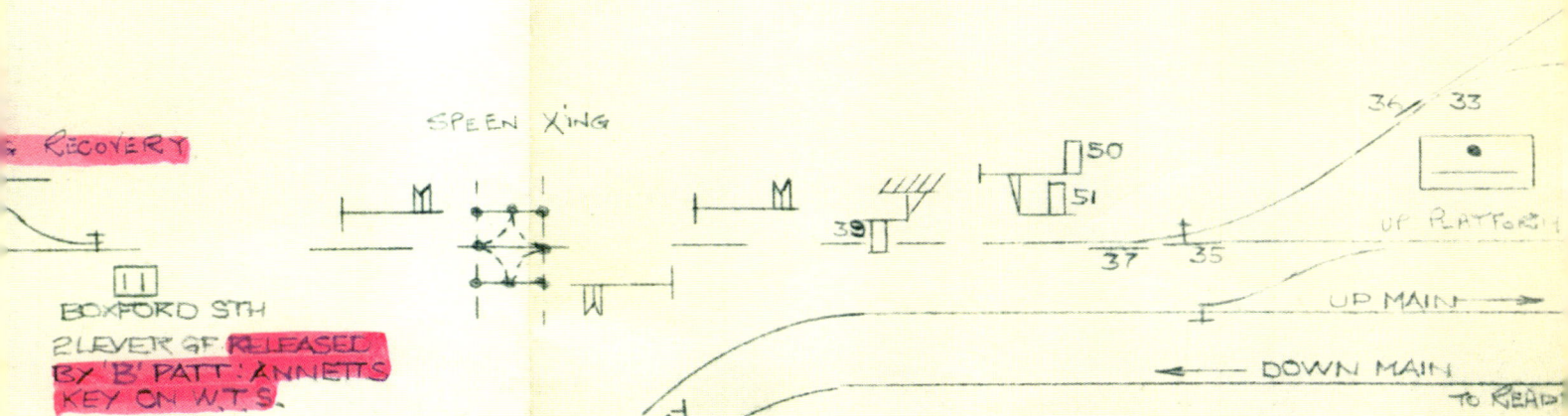

SPEEN XING

RECOVERY

BOXFORD STN
2 LEVER GF RELEASED
BY 'B' PATT. ANNETTS
KEY ON W.T.S.

FROM WESTBURY

39

50
51

36   33

37   35

UP PLATFORM

UP MAIN →

← DOWN MAIN

TO READING

NEWBURY WEST SB.
SPACES 6 8.9 10.11.12.41.42.43.44.45.46

FRAME WK VT 4" CENTRES

OES WORKING TO WELFORD PARK GF

ERS' DRAFT PLAN
DE THEMSELVES ACQUAINTED WITH THE
RES OF THIS SCHEME, RECOMMEND THAT
D OUT AS INDICATED HEREON.

Signature	Date
FOR S STEVENS	29.3.62

LAMBOURN

ERATIONS I/C/W O.E.S. WORKING OF BRANCH

BRITISH RAILWAYS WESTERN REGI
SIGNAL & TELECOMMUNICATIO
ENGINEERING DEPT.,   READI

DRAWN GBC	DATE 15-11-6
CHECKED	DATE 12.1.6
APPROVED	DATE

SP. 61/209/—

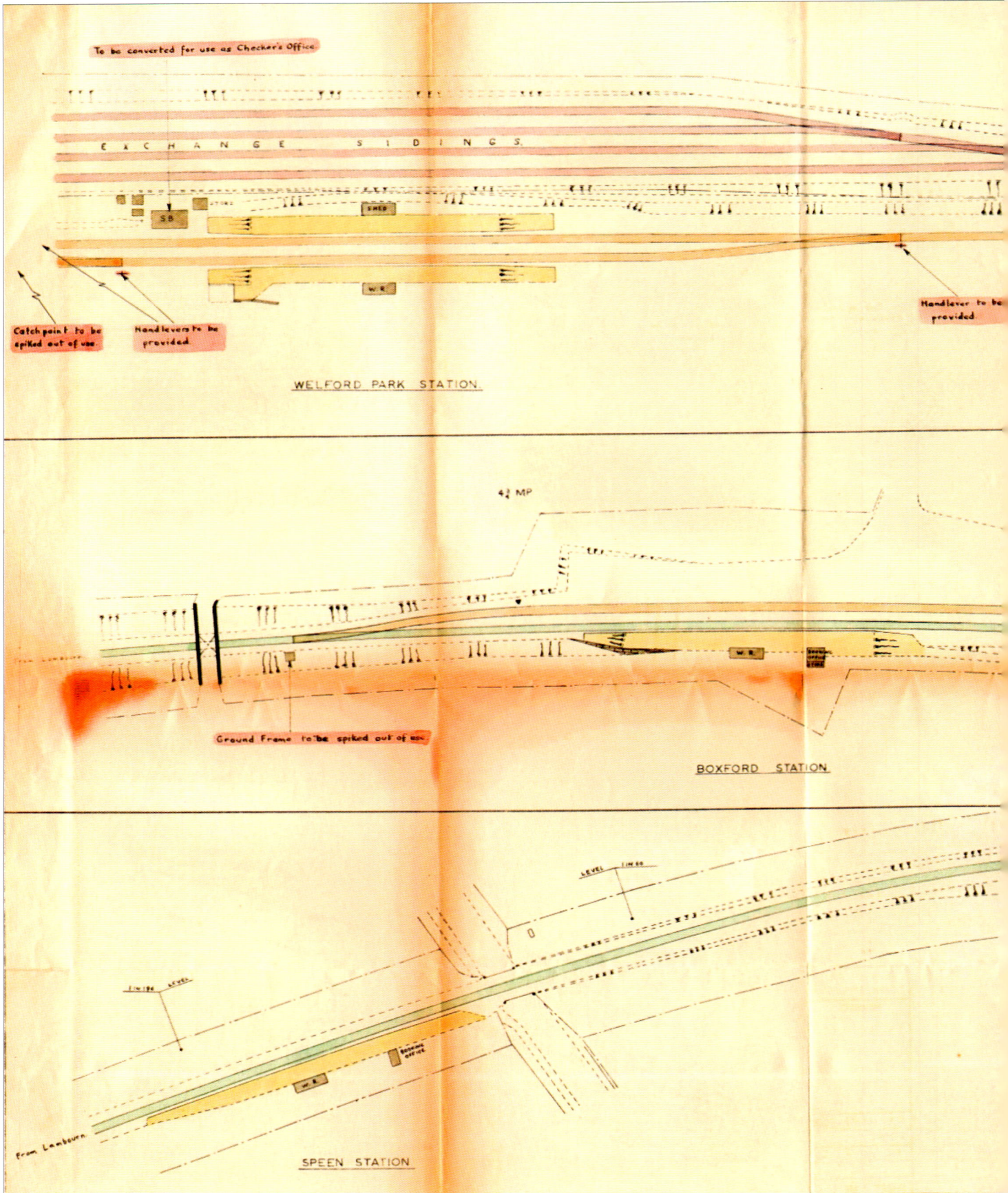

To be converted for use as Checker's Office

E X C H A N G E   S I D I N G S.

S B

SHED

W.R.

Catchpoint to be spiked out of use.

Handlevers to be provided.

Handlever to be provided.

WELFORD PARK STATION.

4½ MP

Ground Frame to be spiked out of use.

W.R.

BOXFORD STATION.

LEVEL   1 IN 66

0

1 IN 164   LEVEL

BOOKING OFFICE

W.R.

from Lambourn.

SPEEN STATION.

Further, slightly more described details of the 1961 economy scheme.

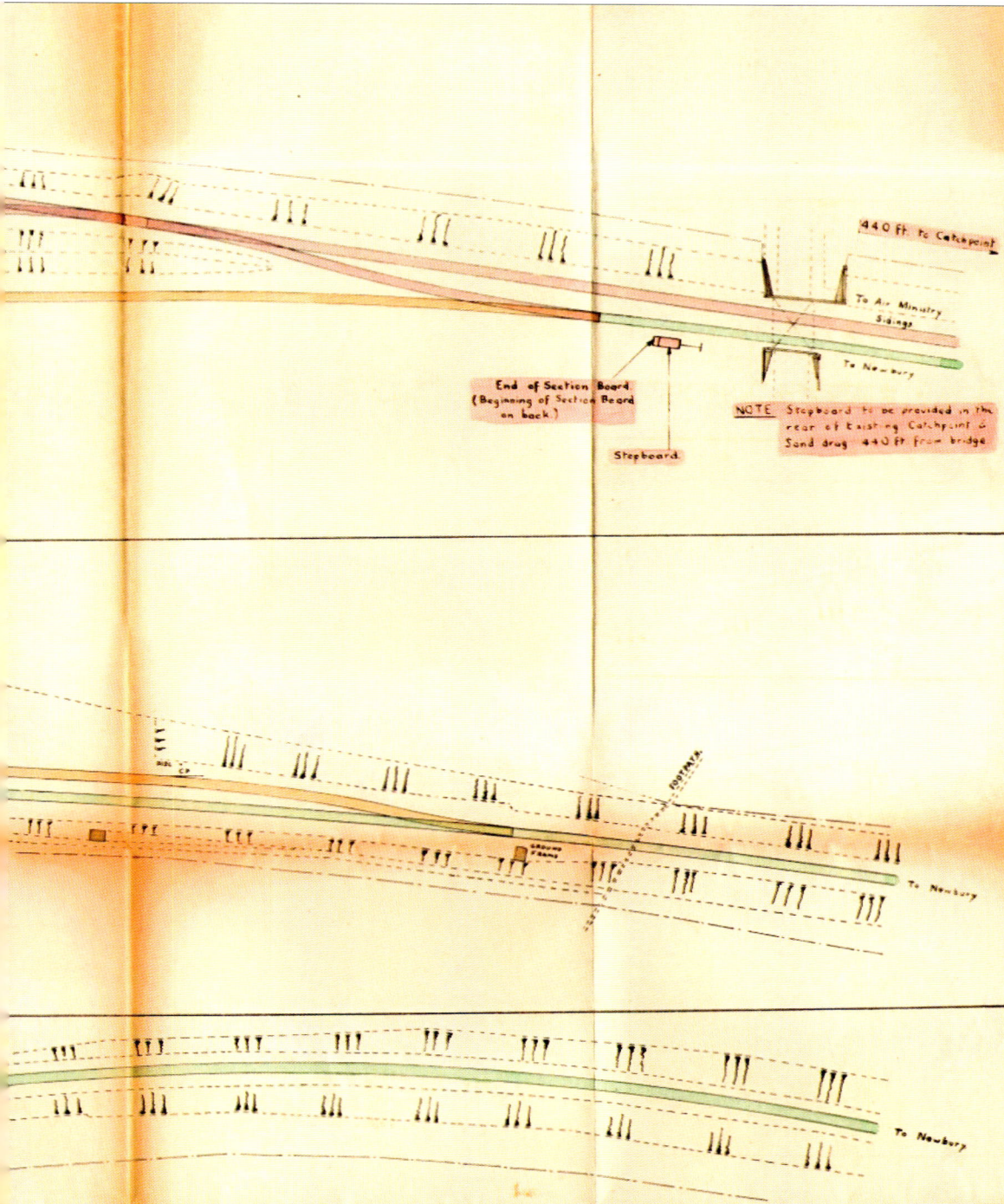

440 ft. to Catchpoint

To Air Ministry Sidings

To Newbury

End of Section Board
(Beginning of Section Board on back.)

NOTE Stopboard to be provided in the rear of Existing Catchpoint & Sand drag 440 ft from bridge.

Stopboard.

To Newbury

To Newbury

DRAFT PLAN

BRITISH RAILWAYS
CIVIL ENGINEER'S DEPT.   DISTRICT ENGINEER'S OFFICE, PADDINGTON.
WESTERN REGION

REVISED

LAMBOURN VALLEY BRANCH.

ALTERATIONS IN CONNECTION WITH U.R.P.S.

STAGE 1. — ONE ENGINE IN STEAM.

OFFICER	SIGNATURE	DATE

SCALES 40 ft. to an inch.

D.E. 905/6 CORR C.E APPROVED FOR STEVENS
R.C.S. R.C.S.
SHEET 1 OF 1. CIVIL ENGINEER

D.E'S No. Q 7995/12797
C.E'S No.

at Newbury might well be used as a substitute for a 22xx from Reading. Whether this was ever actually done is not certain.

On 5th June 1962, BR were now trying to recover those of the costs in operating the line, apportioned to signalman's wages covering the period the 1st July 1954 to the 30th June 1961. Although nowhere is it stated when the new sidings and camp connection were brought into use at Welford, it may be reasonable to assume this was on the first of the two dates mentioned.

A letter was sent to the Air Ministry, requesting payment of £3,758 7s 4d to cover a proportion of the signalman's wages etc at Welford Park. A very rough calculation would indicate that the railway were attempting to recover approximately half of the wage bill for the signalman employed at Welford Park during this period. The result of sending this 'bill' was not recorded.

Not surprisingly, what was an infrequently used railway was also becoming a playground for children and in late 1962 there were several reports of children trespassing at Boxford, having gained access to the site by means of the overbridge at the north end. Officially this bridge was provided for the use of Mr D A Cummins to reach his land on the east side of the railway. A suggestion was made that, by demolishing the bridge, access to the land could be achieved by the former yard entrance. As might be expected there was again no definite decision.

At this stage also the paper trail begins to thin slightly and it is not until mid-June 1963 that the next reference appears. This time it is consideration of complete closure, felt necessary due to bridgework, (the location of which is not specified), in need of heavy repairs in the near future.

As if to underline this view, a note was appended of the amount of munitions traffic despatched during the period May 1962 to April 1963. the total tonnage of this

Month	No of wagons	Destination(s)
May 1962	19	Felixstowe and Prestwick
June	49	Felixstowe, Prestwick and Barry Docks
August	1	Midcalder
September	99	Felixstowe, Prestwick, Barry Docks and Plymouth
October	1	Prestwick
November	29	Felixstowe, Barry Docks and Milford Haven
December	2	Midcalder and Prestwick
February 1963	1	Prestwick
April 1963	51	Prestwick, Barry Docks and Felixstowe.

traffic was 1,470, which was worth £3,812 in revenue. At the same time 24 wagons loads were received from, Felixstowe, Kenilworth, Bedenham, Parkestone Quay, Barry, and Milford Haven, although it is not certain if revenue for this was included in the above figures.

BR were still responsible for maintaining the line, five men being involved, although one was permanently employed as wagon checker at Welford. Employment costs outstripped revenue, it being pointed out that at the end of 1963, revenue from both military and civilian traffic at Welford was £7,000 per annum whilst maintenance costs were £12,500.

The limited volume of military traffic carried thus made a reasonable case for closure on economic grounds. But bearing in mind the potential strategic importance of the route, the Western Region thus approached the Air Ministry to ascertain if they would take over the whole route from Newbury, working it on the basis of a private siding. The response from the USAF came on 3rd January 1964. It stated simply that they were in no position to discuss the matter, an unequivocal end then to the conversation at that point.

The Western Region were left with no alternative, for the present, but to continue to operate the railway. It is not clear what form of requirement existed, but it may be assumed that it was considered to be necessary due to the connection to a military facility. Even so the WR continued to total up the figures, total maintenance expenses for 1963 were put at £450 13 10d, added to which were operating costs of £2,000.

Non military traffic at Welford was also limited by this time. Indeed, in 1963 Welford Park despatched just 6 wagons of merchandise worth just £10, although it did receive 135 valued at £3,400. Additional to this the USAF received 27 and despatched 330. The value of this was an additional £4,190. Mention is also made of a £35 haulage charge. Was this for the hire of an engine, perhaps? During the same period the figures for Boxford were nil, nothing in and nothing out. Stockcross is not even mentioned and it may be assumed then that any race horse traffic had ceased at the same time as the passenger service had been withdrawn. BR figures give the total number of wagons for the line during this period as 498, with revenue at £7,600, although it should be pointed out that these totals do not exactly match the sum of the relevant items.

By the summer of 1963, the working timetable also saw the timings of the public thrice weekly freight altered, so as to leave Newbury at 9.35 am, arriving at Welford Park at 10.15 am. The return departure was 10.40, into Newbury for 11.25 am. The headcode '9A84' applied. This was changed again from the 17th June 1964 to a mid afternoon time. The service would also run on Saturdays if required, each working conveying munitions traffic if necessary, which was not restricted then to complete train loads.

The traffic figures for the six months, January to June 1964, reveal that 76 'civilian' wagons were brought in to Welford, 67 of which were coal. Six were sent out. In addition to this were 230 full wagons and 174 empty wagons arriving for the military and 130 full and 284 empty wagons from the military sent out. As regards special train workings, a total of 36 ran during the whole of 1963 and just 9 in the first six months of 1964.

Meanwhile, with no traffic being handled, it was not surprising that on the 1st December 1964, formal notice was given that, as from the 4th January 1965 freight facilities would be withdrawn from Boxford. No objections were noted. Co-incidentally, the January date was exactly five years since passenger services had been withdrawn. It should also be remembered at this stage that talk of closure of Boxford to goods traffic and the recovery of assets had been rumbling on for some time. As with so many aspects of the final years of the line, it was just another example of indecision.

Meanwhile the attempted sale of the line to the USAF continued and early in 1965 it was reported that

negotiations were indeed taking place, not though between the WR and USAF, but directly between the USAF and British Railways Board.

1965 would be year when the final wagons of public traffic were carried. The physical removal of the siding connection at Boxford on the 1st March was to be expected, but it came as a slight surprise when the Western Region reported that public traffic arriving at Welford was very small, averaging just one wagon per week. Accordingly it was announced that as from 19th July 1965 Welford Park too would close to goods, except to private siding traffic. George Bodman would have to go elsewhere for his coal.

Interestingly, in October 1965 the WR were once again brought in to negotiations with the USAF, acting it now appears through the Ministry of Defence. It would seem that the MoD had heard nothing from BRB about taking over the route and were asking advice as to whom they should contact! In fact, no decision was made until

GOVERNMENT TRAFFIC					
1963	Days Operated	Trips Run	Loaded Wagons	Average per day Operated	Actual trip run - all traffic
January	-	-	-	-	5
February	2	2	6	3	9
March	-	-	-	-	8
April	5	5	16	3	9
May	2	2	3	1	10
June	5	5	9	2	8
July	5	8	85	17	13
August	1	1	2	2	7
September	2	2	4	2	7
October	2	2	1	-	7
November	3	5	40	13	12
December	9	20	191	21	20
	36	52	357	10	115

Civilian			Depot		
	Coal	Goods	Explosives	Empties	Total
Inwards	92	46	330	50	518
Outwards	-	6	27	485*	518
*Estimated	92	52	357	535	1036

Government Traffic Received		Government Traffic Forwarded		
	1962	1963	1962	1963	
Wagons	26	330	226	27	
Total	101	1525	1507	127	

Replacement for the 22xx steam locomotives used, were the BR D63xx Diesel Hydraulic type. D6343 seen waiting for the gates to be opened at Speen on the way to Welford.

October 1966, when it was finally announced that the USAF were not interested in purchasing the line but would consider a lease.

From mid 1965 onwards, the only traffic that could be counted in relation to the railway, was in the form of military traffic, the estimate for the year being that 404 loaded wagons were dealt with. From this time it appears any traffic was sporadic. A report of 18 months later, probably applying to the years 1965/66 generally, commented that military traffic was sometimes carried on four separate days a week, but then a month would then pass before there was any further movement.

Generally too, road was beginning to be perceived as having preference to rail, the local consequence of this coming at the start of 1967 and the proposed new east – west motorway, later designated the M4. The route of the road would mean bridging the railway which of course did eventually occur. At the same time BR took pains to point out to the Ministry of Transport that their plan for another overbridge crossing over the Didcot - Newbury line was unnecessary. This route having closed completely in 1964.

The use of Welford Park as a potential railhead for

offloading concrete sections necessary for the motorway / railway bridge and as a railhead for roadstone trains was also discussed. Whether either took place is not certain, although in the latter case the estimate was for some 5-7 trains of 1,000 tons weekly for up to six months. As a train of this weight was beyond the capability of a Class 22 (D63xx) locomotive, it was suggested that each 38 wagon train of stone be split at Newbury and taken to Welford in two halves, the former goods siding being used for unloading. Even so, it would have been necessary for a member of staff to open the gates at Speen crossing in advance, so avoiding a train of such weight having to stop on the 1 in 60 rise leading to the level crossing. Understandably, the Ministry of Defence were contacted over the proposal and were reported as having no objections, provided their own traffic was not interfered with. A sop from BR was that any charges currently in place for rental of the branch would be suspended during the period the stone trains were in operation.

Possibly in connection with the lease / rental of the line by the military authorities, (both words are used in correspondence), in February 1967 the Civil Engineer produced a report on the value of the line. It was reported the trackwork was worth £57,530 and the bridges £13,980 Annual maintenance, including ditches, fences and roads, £2,875. Annual renewal costs were put at £935.

At the same time, figures for military traffic carried in 1966, the first full year when this was the only traffic using the line, were revealed. 2,708 tons of goods had been received and 5,086 tons forwarded. This involved a total of 88 wagons. No BR engines were hired in 1966. Incoming traffic had been received from Bishopton, Longtown, Milford Haven, Felixstowe, and Chorley. Outgoing traffic was forwarded to Milford Haven, Barry Docks and Felixstowe.

The above information is then contradicted in another document, possible more accurate, which gives details for January to November showing that, in 12 trains, 357 wagons were received. Total revenue was £12,390, which included seven trains despatched plus a further 21 to RAF Chilmark. It was noted that the latter movement was due to the complete removal of RAF stores and was unlikely to occur again.

The scrap value of the railway was put at £10,800 and the value of the land at a further £2,000. At the same time, BR now gave the USAF the approximate annual costs of both maintaining and running the railway. A lease was offered at £1,250 pa or an alternative purchase price of £75,000. Annual renewal and maintenance costs of £4,100 p.a. were open to discussion, giving the impression that BR wanted to get rid of the route.

The result was that the Air Ministry at last realised that they had little option but to take over the line themselves, should they wish to ensure a continuity of operation. Accordingly, on the 2nd March 1967, the Air Ministry agreed to the leasing of the railway, although with the proviso that BR were to provide locomotives. The Air

With the second man having opened the gates, the train will now draw forward until ready to stop whereupon the Guard will close the gates ready for pedestrians and road traffic to proceed. Long periods of inactivity on the line by the late 1960's meant the passage of a train was sometimes seen as something quite unusual.

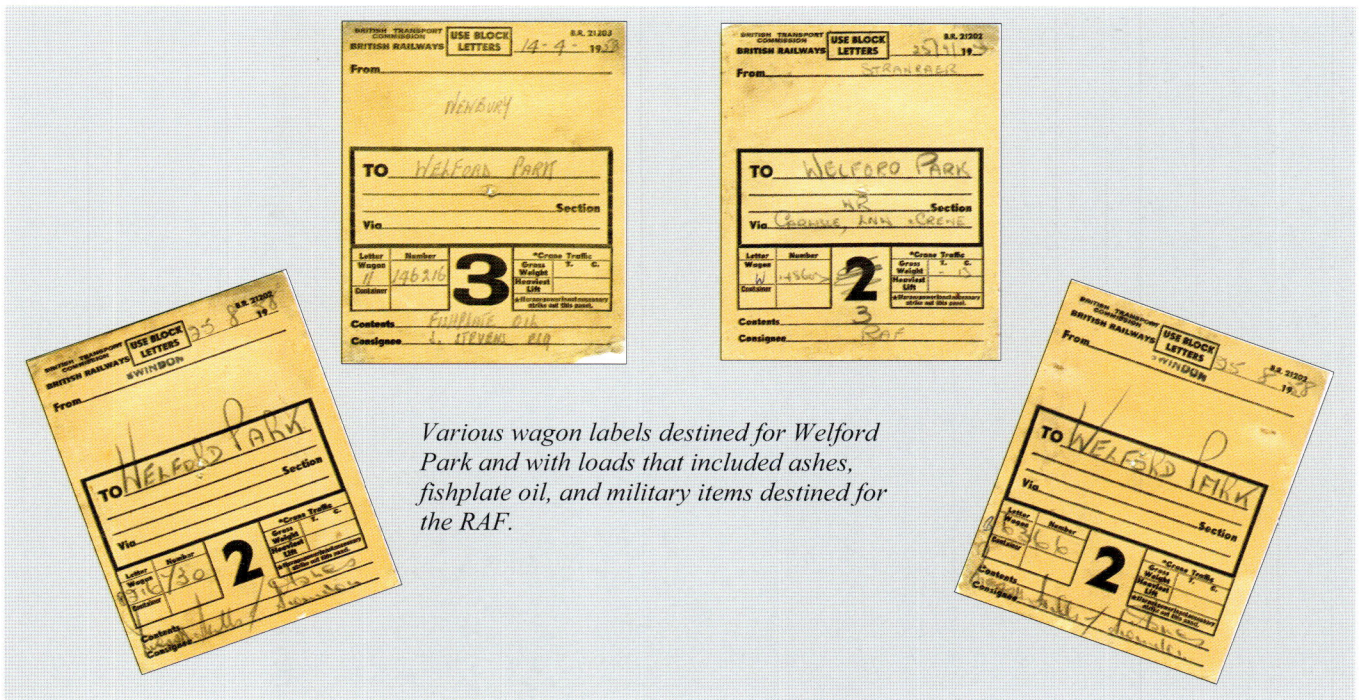

Various wagon labels destined for Welford Park and with loads that included ashes, fishplate oil, and military items destined for the RAF.

The return trip, again at Speen and preparing to cross what is still known as Station Road today. It is not believed any military traffic to or from Welford ran during night hours. The site of the station is now marked by a private development with the somewhat unusual spelling of 'The Sydings'.

Ministry also noted that the stated maintenance costs quoted were too high, as in other areas (it was not stated where), the cost for maintenance was £2 per yard. The final item in the file was a scheduled meeting sometime in April 1967, to finalise details with the USAAF itself.

Whether this mention of BR locomotives working the line was a permanent arrangement is also not certain, as on occasions a green and red liveried 'Army' 350 hp diesel shunter would venture to Newbury to collect and deliver wagons from and to Newbury goods yard.

From 1967, the route passed away from BR control. Even so, the Air Ministry appeared not to realise the full potential of the route, as munitions traffic would also arrive at Welford base having come direct by road. Presumably goods were shipped out in the same way? Thus, for the final six years of operation, from 1967 to 1973, rail traffic to and from Welford was at best sporadic. Despite this, the route appears to have been reasonably maintained, presumably by BR. It was likely though that this was just day to day work, weed control, hedge cutting, point oiling etc. Certainly there is no evidence of any major renewals during this period. Some concrete sleepered track was in place at odd locations near Boxford at least. When this was laid out is not known.

The provision of an access road to the military depot off the eastbound carriageway of M4 also contributed to the end of necessary rail requirements. Road was ever more the favoured option and it would appear that whilst officially the railway was still operational, traffic was ever more limited.

Here matters rested until 1973, when either the Ministry or BR, we do not know which, decided the route was no longer viable. Possibly it was a combination of both, road being preferred to rail and necessary renewals deemed cost-prohibitive.

Formal notice was thus given to close the route, but before this occurred the Western Region agreed to a send-off in style, with the well known 'Last Train to Welford' excursions of November 1973. Other special enthusiasts trains had also used the route at intervals prior to this time but usually only carrying specific groups rarely associated with the Newbury area.

Just before November 1973, it looked as if there was a possibility of a reprieve, a letter appearing on file, from a Mr Pullen of Slough, enquiring about the purchase of the line for a future preservation attempt. (It is believed the Great Western Society also expressed an interest in the route at some time.) BR's internal response was that the Chief Civil Engineer had undertaken a survey of the line, confirming that by now the majority of the track was of scrap value only. In addition, much of the bridgework was in such poor condition that BR main line locomotives would be prohibited from crossing them. This gives credence to the previously held assumption, that BR locomotives may have ceased using the line sometime before 1973. There were additional factors, one being that the Western Region intended to retain a short stub of the branch at the Newbury end for the purpose of stabling 12 coach trains from Newbury Racecourse. It is not believed that this was ever done, but it did mean that at the time there was not the potential for trains to run directly into Newbury. Various parties (unspecified) had also expressed interest in purchasing individual pockets of land, whilst current legislation also required that British Railways first offer the complete line to Berkshire County Council.

In addition to Mr Pullen's interest, there was at the time a very serious interest by Berkshire County Council in taking over the line, which it appears BR were already aware of. Indeed BR's suggestion was that they understood the Council might well be looking into purchase and subsequent leasing to a private operator and this was communicated to Mr Pullen, possibly in the hope that the various parties might liaise accordingly. Even so, the matter of access to Newbury station was still an issue, although

Following prolonged periods of inactivity, the initiative of the Western Region in running four special trains was commendable. Even if this were indeed to be the very end of the branch, it would still be interesting to learn of the behind the scenes planning that must have taken place in order to allow the operation of the trains.

As part of the planning exercise inspection of the track and structures must have taken place and it may be realistically concluded that up to this time, at least, the route had remained in fair condition. That is not to say that major work might not have been deemed necessary shortly afterwards, had services of any type been retained.

The day was well publicised locally and consequently patronage was excellent. BR even organised a sale of various items of 'Railwayana' at Newbury on the day. The trains also featured on local television news reports that evening whilst the event was subsequently well covered in the local press.

Different colour tickets were issued relative to the differing times of train run, each ticket allowing just one return trip.

LAMBOURN VALLEY FAREWELL
SATURDAY 3 NOVEMBER
SPECIAL TRAINS
will run from
NEWBURY TO WELFORD PARK & Return
Depart NEWBURY at
09 45   11 40   13 40   15 40
Fare 60p adult or child

Please send me ____ tickets @ 60p each for the Lambourn Valley Farewell. I will be travelling on the ____*train from Newbury.
I enclose cheque/P.O. for £ _____   *Please insert time of train
Name _____   and an alternative here ____
Address _____
Please send this form with your remittance and an s.a.e. to:
British Rail, CP 27, Western Tower, Reading RG1 1NQ, Berkshire.

Special working passing over the canal bridge on 3rd November 1975. Two three car DMU sets were used for the service.

David Cooper / Courtesy A .A. Cundick

2nd - CHEAP DAY
FAREWELL TO THE
LAMBOURN VALLEY RAILWAY
3rd November, 1973
Newbury to
WELFORD PARK
AND BACK
Valid by 11·45 train only
(W)   For conditions see over
0347

26th May 1973 and a view from the canal bridge over the Kennet and Avon north towards Speen. The switchback nature of parts the route is also visible, and so is the seemingly well maintained permanent way.

David Cooper / Courtesy A .A. Cundick

BR did not now seems to rule this out completely if the Council were involved.

Whilst, no doubt, discussion took place within the County Council, BR were attempting to force the issue, by setting a date of the 1st April 1974, after which time they would start to charge interest on the value of the assets.

That the Council's intentions were serious is not in doubt, for costings were prepared for restoration of the line, to make it suitable for either a peak hour or a full daily service, together with likely annual operating costs and even timetables. The latter included a maximum 14 trains each way daily, between Newbury and Welford Park, commencing at 6.25 am and running through until 10.30 pm. Throughout the day these were timed to fit in with the existing main line service. Dependent upon the level of service to be operated, either a single coach or three coach DMU would be involved. BR had confirmed by now that whilst the track in the former Lambourn bay at Newbury had by now been lifted, it could be reinstated if necessary.

The task facing the County Council was to stimulate rail travel to attempt to reduce road congestion in Newbury. In these respects the idea was well in the forefront of what is now the environmental agenda, although at the time it must be said that only the local impact was being considered and not the potential of attracting commuters from the M4. by means of a 'Park and Ride' at Welford.

A final decision was reached in May 1975, with the note that the Council considered the benefits did not outweigh the costs. No mention was made of Mr Pullen at this stage. Perhaps the final irony was that, after this, BR then attempted to pursue the Council with a view to a possible re-opening instead for freight! What type and for what purpose cannot be imagined, as the USAF had indicated there was no possibility of a return to rail usage. Understandably, nothing further is heard of this final comment although it seems BR were ever hopeful and again delayed a final decision on recovery of the track for another three weeks.

Eventually, on the 3rd July 1975, with no likelihood of future freight or passenger traffic, authorisation was finally given for the removal of the track. Whether this was carried out by BR or by contractor is uncertain, although as far as the railway was concerned there was a value of £100,900 in scrap materials set against £17,100 as the cost of recovery. We have no date for when this actually took place, although the final page of the file, dated October 1976, stated that work was 'in hand' and scheduled to be finished by December 1976. Subsequently the land was also sold.

So far as the military sidings at Welford were concerned and the actual route to the base, there is perhaps understandably, no information concerning their removal and recovery. For some years afterwards it was possible to see part of the course of the line, where it curved around alongside the M4. But, as with the parts of the original route, much has reverted to farmland, or in other locations been the subject of development. Two tangible assets do remain. One the former waiting shelter from Boxford, which still does service as a bus shelter, on the old main

Opposite top - The approach to Welford, following the removal and recovery of the signalling equipment. The notice seen was of the type provided in July 1962. This undated view depicts rusted rails, although on paper the line was still open for military traffic.
Opposite lower - From part way up the gradient, a view of the end of the sand-drag leading down from the camp is obtained. Whether the sand-drag consisted of similar trackwork throughout its length is not certain. The warning board seen in the top view is also visible on the right.

road near the station and, of course the Ticket Office from Welford, lovingly restored as a exhibit at Didcot Railway Centre.

Thus ends what is literally the final chapter in the history of the Lambourn line, which by co-incidence only just managed to reach it's centenary, given that it was in 1873 that the first proposals for a connection from Lambourn were suggested.

In its brief life as an independent company, it probably projected a colourful appearance, although those who had both invested in and managed it quickly came to realise that it was never likely to be anything other than a financial drain. Under the Great Western, modernised and upgraded, it served as a typical rural byway, just about covering its operating costs, at a time when there was little competition for traffic and wage rates had not escalated as in later years.

It was inflation following the second world war that really saw the start of the difficulties and in some respects the line came perilously close to being one of the first closure casualties, of what was by then the nationalised railway network. At the time, its saviour was undoubtedly the new sidings and connection at Welford. Even so the new facility hardly appeared to have been fully utilised, but whether was through lack of communication, expectation, or purely on the basis of economics cannot be confirmed. Instead, any advantage, both in convenience of traffic and financial gain, came in fits and starts, whilst, during the lulls, operating and maintenance costs still accrued.

What is so sad is the way the railway initially attempted to manipulate receipts in order to prove their own case for closure. Maintenance is another factor, which is rarely discussed in the various line histories that have been written, but it must be said that a reduction in maintenance levels over the years could only have one eventual outcome, a time when safety of operation were compromised due to the prevailing condition of the infrastructure. Even so, we do know that, despite their protestations towards hardship, BR did relay sections of the route towards Welford with concrete sleepers, although at whose expense is not recorded.

The farcical situation in the early years, when the USAF seemed to have no knowledge that a rail link was available, could hardly be imagined and of course the question has to be, how much traffic was lost over the years, through what can only be described as pure ignorance?

Then there was the inaction by BR over seemingly simple changes. Why did it take three years to reduce the signalling after 1960 is just one of the questions. There are many more, both before and after that one.

On the very last day, the running of the special trains to commemorate closure was a wonderful public relations coup by the Western Region. Those responsible were Frank Dumbleton, Andrew Emmerson, and Gordon Rushton. Having missed the opportunity for a brake-van trip in 1971, I was also away from the area in 1973 and only ever heard of the last day workings subsequently. After that time it is not believed any rail vehicle ever used the line.

The behaviour of the County Council has previously been referred to as commendable and that view will not be altered here. What is perhaps a pity is how those concerned with local road congestion at the time could not have foreseen the gridlock that now exists everywhere, not withstanding the rocketing price of fossil based fuels. The potential for a 'Park and Ride' facility, with direct access off the M4 on the site of the military sidings at Welford Park, would have been ideal for private vehicles, but was lost. To achieve this in 1974/5 would have been beyond the remit of the local council and the then Ministry of Transport would have had to become involved.

So the Lambourn line commenced, existed and died in the same form, a rural railway throughout.

SHUNTING GOODS TRAINS ON TO LAMBOURN BRANCH NEWBURY WEST BOX.

After the last Train has arrived at Welford Park, and the tablet at the station has been restored to the instrument, the Signalman at Newbury West Box must send the "Release tablet for shunting purposes" Signal to Welford Park, and a tablet must be withdrawn and kept out of the instrument until the opening time of the Branch on the following morning.

Goods Trains may be shunted from the UP Platform Line to the Lambourn Branch as required whilst the tablet is out of the instrument. The Line falls towards Newbury, and care must be taken to secure the wagons if the Engine is withdrawn.

A red tail light must always be exhibited when a Train is placed on the Lambourn Branch, and when the Engine is not on the Train a red head light must also be shewn.

Except when required to be handed to the driver of a Goods Train shunted on to the Lambourn Branch, the tablet must be securely locked up in a drawer in the Signal Box, and when the Welford Park Box is opened the tablet must be restored to the instrument and the "Shunting completed Tablet replaced" Signal must be sent to Welford Park, but before doing so the Signalman at Newbury West Box must obtain an assurance from the Shunter that the Branch Line is absolutely clear.

The arrangement is not to apply to "Dead" Trains or to odd vehicles.

LAMBOURN VALLEY LINE.

There are three Public Road Crossings where Gatemen are in charge by day, viz., Speen, Bockhampton and East Garston; Speen Crossing is at Speen Station, Bockhampton is about one mile the south side of Lambourn Station and East Garston at East Garston Station. There are no fixed Signals, but the gates are provided with targets and lamps which show a green light in each direction when the gates are closed across the public road and a red target by day and red light by night when across the Railway. Drivers must approach both crossings cautiously and be prepared to stop if gates are across the Railway. All Trains running between 8.0 p.m. and 7.0 a.m. must stop. The gates must be unlocked and opened by the Fireman, and when the Train is clear of the crossing the Guard will shut and lock the gates across the Railway.

(Clearly the mention of there being any fixed signals at the crossings did not take into account the provision of the distant signals in 1957.)

WORKING THE GROUND FRAMES AT BOXFORD, WELFORD PARK, GREAT SHEFFORD AND EAST GARSTON.

1. The Frame controlling the Siding Points is locked by the Electric Tablet.

2. The Porter in charge will he held responsible when on duty for seeing that the whole of the work is properly performed and that the Tablet is handed back to the Engineman after the necessary work has been done, the Points properly set and the Ground Frame locked.

3. The Guard in charge of the Train will in a like manner be responsible when the Porter is off duty and before giving the "Right away" Signal to the Driver must satisfy himself that the work is complete and that the Tablet has been handed back to the Engineman.

INSTRUCTIONS FOR WORKING LAMBOURN VALLEY BRANCH, SUNDAYS.

1. On Sundays, until further notice, the Electric Train Tablet working will be withdrawn in connection with the ordinary Sunday Train Service, and Trains over the Branch worked by Pilotman in accordance with the Regulations for working Single Lines by Pilot Guard, shewn on page 78 of the General Appendix to the Book of Rules and Regulations.

2. A Relief Signalman provided by the District Inspector, and appointed by the person in charge at Newbury Station, must act as Pilotman and wear a badge.

3. The Pliotman must take charge of the Tablet, which will be withdrawn by Newbury West Box Signalman for shunting purposes in accordance with the Regulations shewn on page 57 of this Book for the Section Newbury to Welford Park. (See Clause 5 below.)

4. The Points at Welford Park must be set for the Down Line and Signals lowered for that direction, and the trailing points clipped and padlocked before the Signalman leaves duty on Saturday nights.

Signals for the Up Line which must be maintained at danger are to be passed in such position by the Driver on the authority of the Pilotman.

5. Before leaving duty on Saturday night (except when a Special Train is being run over the Branch on the following day, see paragraph 15), the Welford Park Signalman must withdraw a Tablet for the Welford Park and Lambourn Section from the instrument. This Tablet to be used by the Pilotman on Sunday, and replaced in the instrument by him on arrival at Welford Park on the return journey from Lambourn.

The Lambourn Signalman (except as provided for in Clause 15 below) must before leaving duty on Saturday night, set the road and lower Signals for the Train coming from Welford Park. The Pilotman must set the road and lower Signals at Lanbourn for return Train.

6. The Pilotman must obtain a Signal Box key from Newbury West Box, to open the Boxes on the Branch as may be necessary.

7. The Trainmen will be responsible for opening and closing the Level Crossing Gates at Speen, East Garston and Bockhampton.

8. In case of a breakdown the Pilotman must proceed to the most convenient place where communication for assistance can be sent.

9. Except at Lambourn and Great Shefford there will be no Staff on duty at the Stations on the Branch on Sundays, and the Guard must be supplied with an excess pad and particulars of the fares, by the person in charge at Newbury, and must issue tickets to passengers from Branch Stations to Branch Stations or Newbury. Passengers for Stations beyond Newbury must be instructed to re-book at that Station.

10. The Guard must take particulars of all milk churns loaded into the Train at each Station where there is no Staff on duty on the form provided, and hand the form to the appointed person at Newbury with the consignment notes. He must also pay in the fares collected to the Booking Clerk. The Station Master to arrange for sending Stations to be advised of the milk forwarded, by first Train on Monday mornings, in order that the waybills may be prepared without delay.

11. The Pilotman must assist the Guard in dealing with milk and luggage at each Station.

12. Any horses which may be conveyed on the Train for a Station where no Staff is on duty must be unloaded on the Platform and the empty boxes taken through to Lambourn.

Any empty horse boxes for Stations on the Branch must he put off at the Station concerned.

Parcels for Stations on the Branch, with the exception of Great Shefford and Lambourn, must he held back for first Train on Monday morning-

13. When necessary, Platform Lamps to be lighted by the Guard and Pilotman on the forward journey and extinguished before leaving on the return trip.

14. On arrival at Newbury on the return journey Pilot working must be cancelled, and the Pilotman must return the Tablet and Signal Box key to the Signalman in Newbury West Box.

15. When it is necessary to run a Special Train on the Branch with Race Horse Traffic on Sundays, the Station Master at Lambourn must arrange for the Staff to be booked on duty at the Stations concerned to deal with the Special, and after the Train has cleared, the Branch must be closed and the Staff booked off, the arrangements set out above being carried out in connection with the regular booked service. When the Special is run before the booked Sunday Train the Signalmen at Welford Park and Lambourn, before leaving duty, must arrange in accordance with Clauses 4 and 5 of these Instructions.

(The reference to milk is interesting as this was never a major source of revenue for the line).

Ironically these instructions appear in the Western Region Sectional Appendix for May 1960 - *five months after the route north of Welford had closed!*

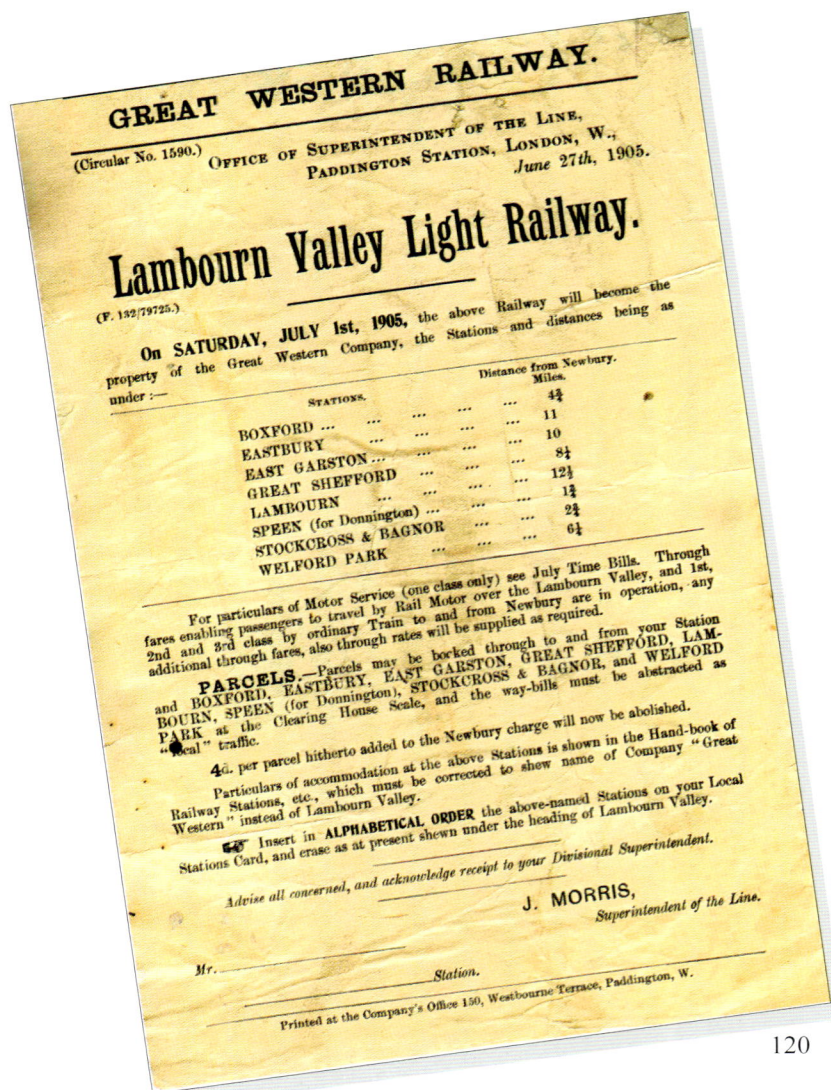

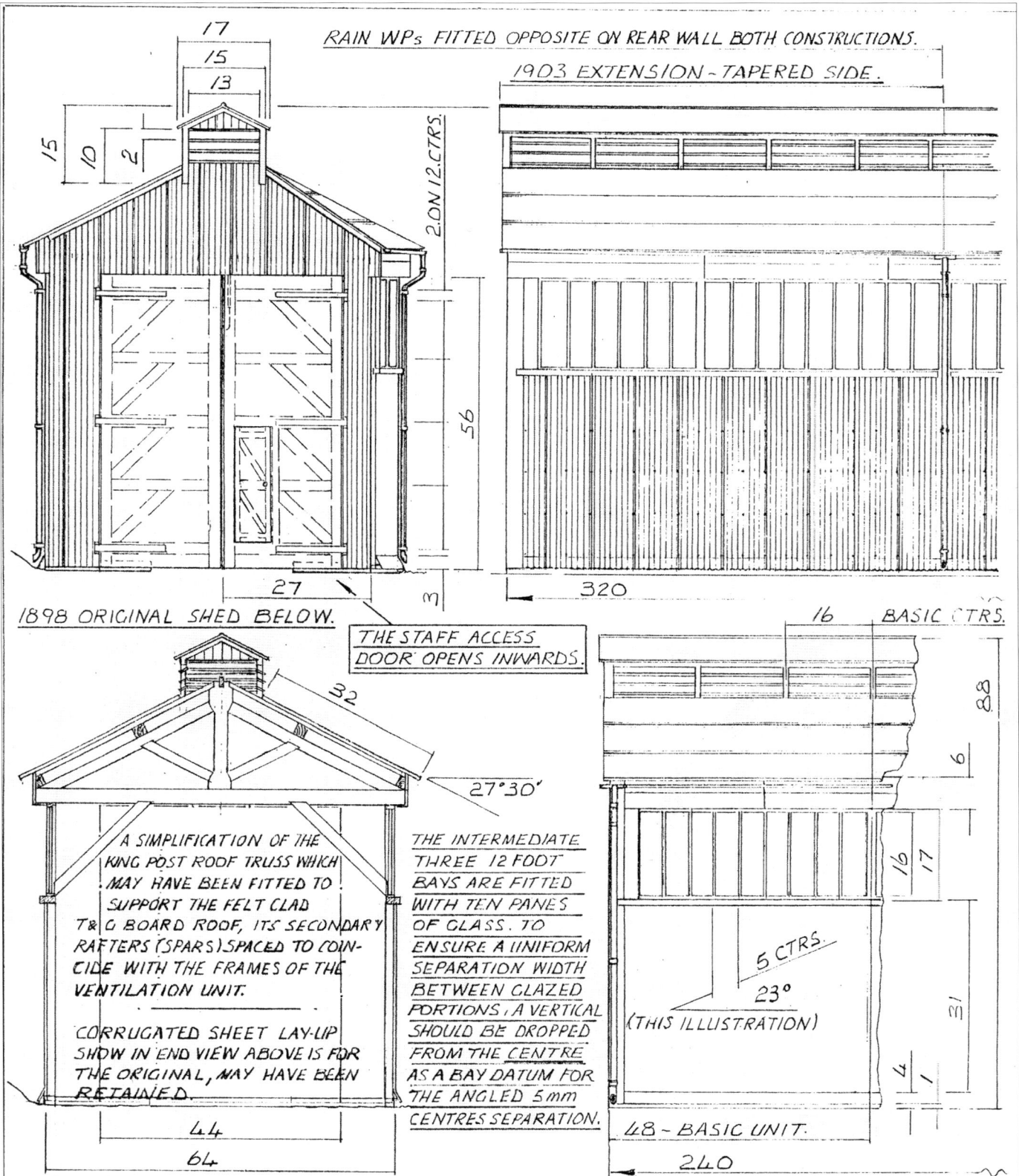

RAIN WPs FITTED OPPOSITE ON REAR WALL BOTH CONSTRUCTIONS.

1903 EXTENSION - TAPERED SIDE.

17
15
13

15
10
2

2 ON 12 CTRS.

56

27

3

1898 ORIGINAL SHED BELOW.

THE STAFF ACCESS DOOR OPENS INWARDS.

320

16   BASIC CTRS.

88

6

32

27°30'

A SIMPLIFICATION OF THE KING POST ROOF TRUSS WHICH MAY HAVE BEEN FITTED TO SUPPORT THE FELT CLAD T&G BOARD ROOF, ITS SECONDARY RAFTERS (SPARS) SPACED TO COIN-CIDE WITH THE FRAMES OF THE VENTILATION UNIT.

CORRUGATED SHEET LAY-UP SHOW IN END VIEW ABOVE IS FOR THE ORIGINAL, MAY HAVE BEEN RETAINED.

THE INTERMEDIATE THREE 12 FOOT BAYS ARE FITTED WITH TEN PANES OF GLASS. TO ENSURE A UNIFORM SEPARATION WIDTH BETWEEN GLAZED PORTIONS, A VERTICAL SHOULD BE DROPPED FROM THE CENTRE AS A BAY DATUM FOR THE ANGLED 5mm CENTRES SEPARATION.

16
17

5 CTRS
23°
(THIS ILLUSTRATION)

31

4
1

44

64

48 - BASIC UNIT.

240

LAMBOURN VALLEY RAILWAY; LAMBOURN ENGINE SHED 1898-1937.
DRAWN AT 4mm TO THE FOOT.   REFERENCES - TLB ρ 13.14.16.103 & 116.   JSP. 27/6/86.

LAMBOURN VALLEY RAILWAY - ENGINE SHED 1898-1903.

A number of official GWR drawings, including those appertaining to the water supply at Lambourn survive in the Wiltshire County Record Office at Trowbridge. Water supply plans often include number of interesting features whilst in addition there is a GWR plan of the locomotive shed, an extract from which is shown as the smaller view above. The danger from taking any such plan, including this one as 'definite', is in relation to changes that may have been made on the ground, either at the time of building, or subsequently. The plan itself is dated as late as April 1934, by which time the actual building had been in existence for 36 years having also been extended since 1898. What we cannot be certain of, is if this was a copy of an earlier drawing, or was based on an actual site survey from 1934? There would also appear to be some disparity between that shown and the drawing on page 121. This applies particularly to the roof supports, but again were they omitted on one drawing perhaps purely for the sake of clarity? We know the engine shed had been removed by about 1939, what we do not know is if there was ever any intention of retaining it and even having a diesel railcar out-stationed at Lambourn. Within the shed, any stores kept would have been notional, oil, rags etc. Similarly, during the time a locomotive was stabled at Lambourn it is likely there must have some provision for coaling but details of this have not been accurately established.

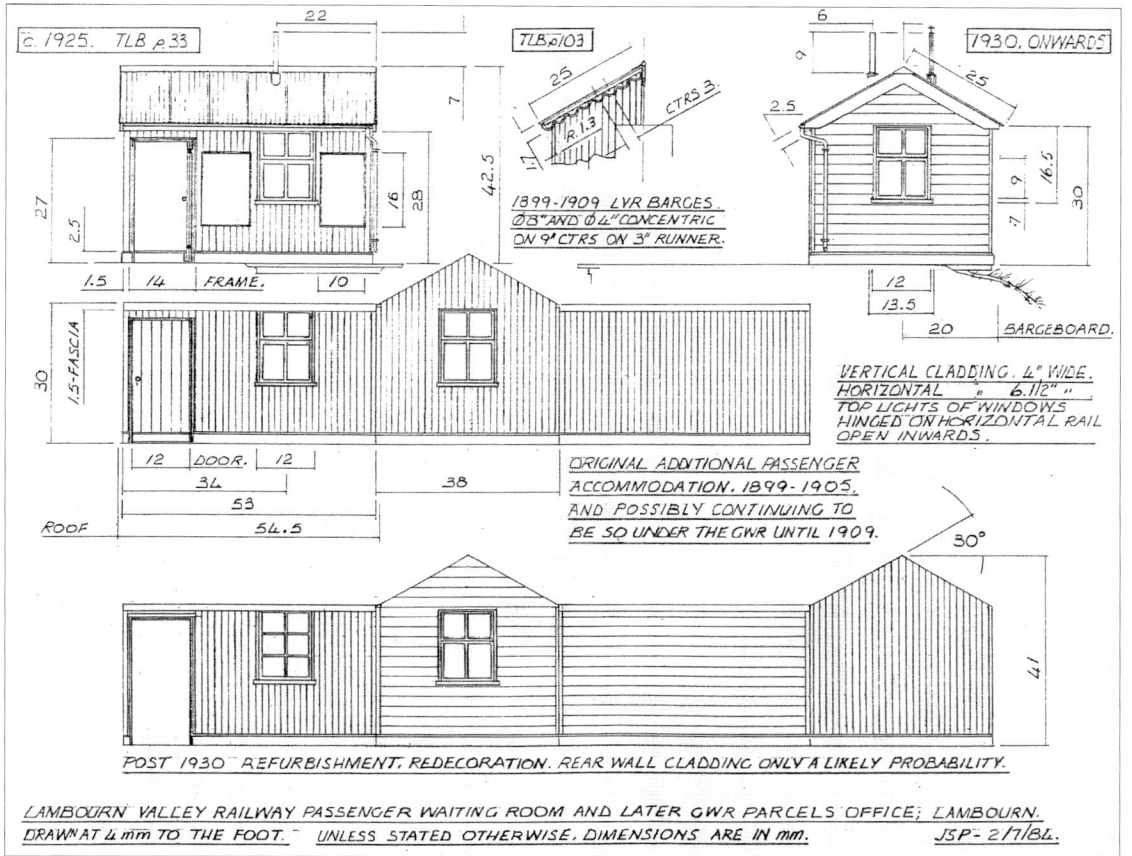

LAMBOURN VALLEY RAILWAY PASSENGER WAITING ROOM AND LATER GWR PARCELS OFFICE; LAMBOURN.
DRAWN AT 4 mm TO THE FOOT. UNLESS STATED OTHERWISE, DIMENSIONS ARE IN mm. JSP- 2/7/84.

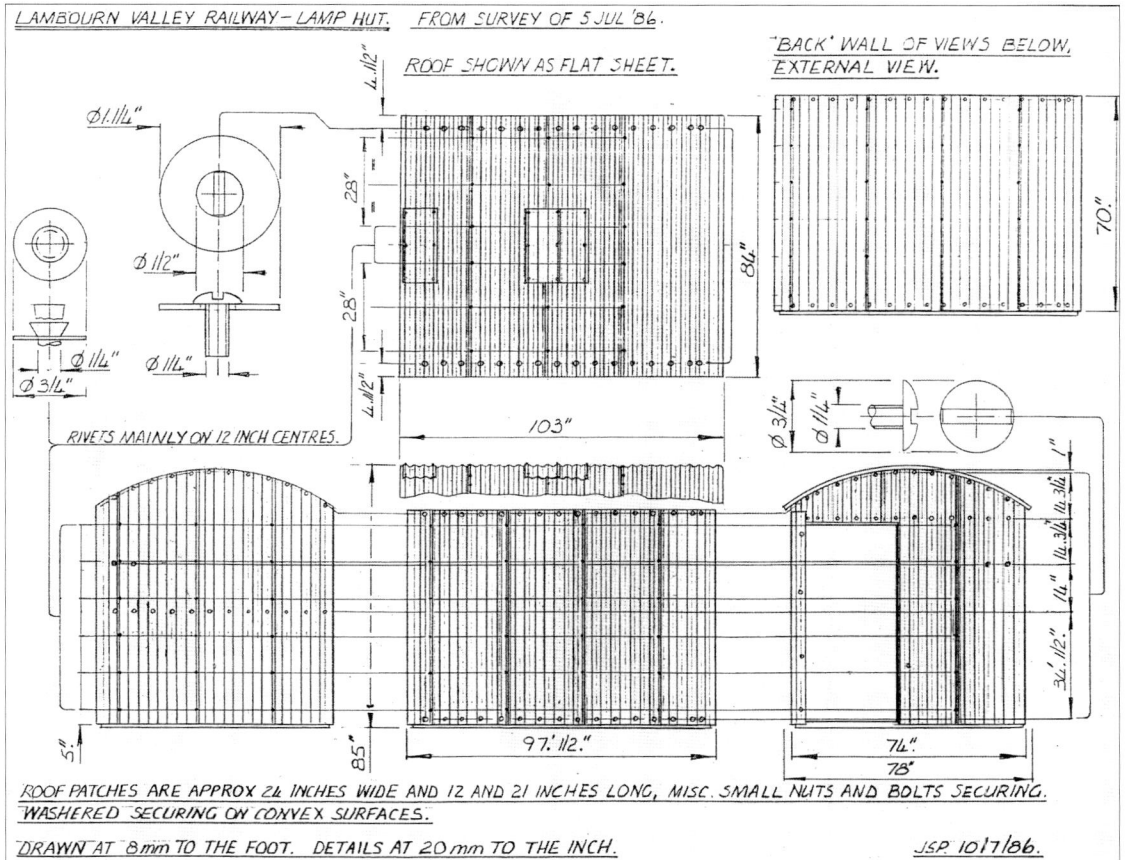

ROOF PATCHES ARE APPROX 24 INCHES WIDE AND 12 AND 21 INCHES LONG, MISC. SMALL NUTS AND BOLTS SECURING.
WASHERED SECURING ON CONVEX SURFACES.

DRAWN AT 8mm TO THE FOOT. DETAILS AT 20 mm TO THE INCH. JSP 10/7/86.

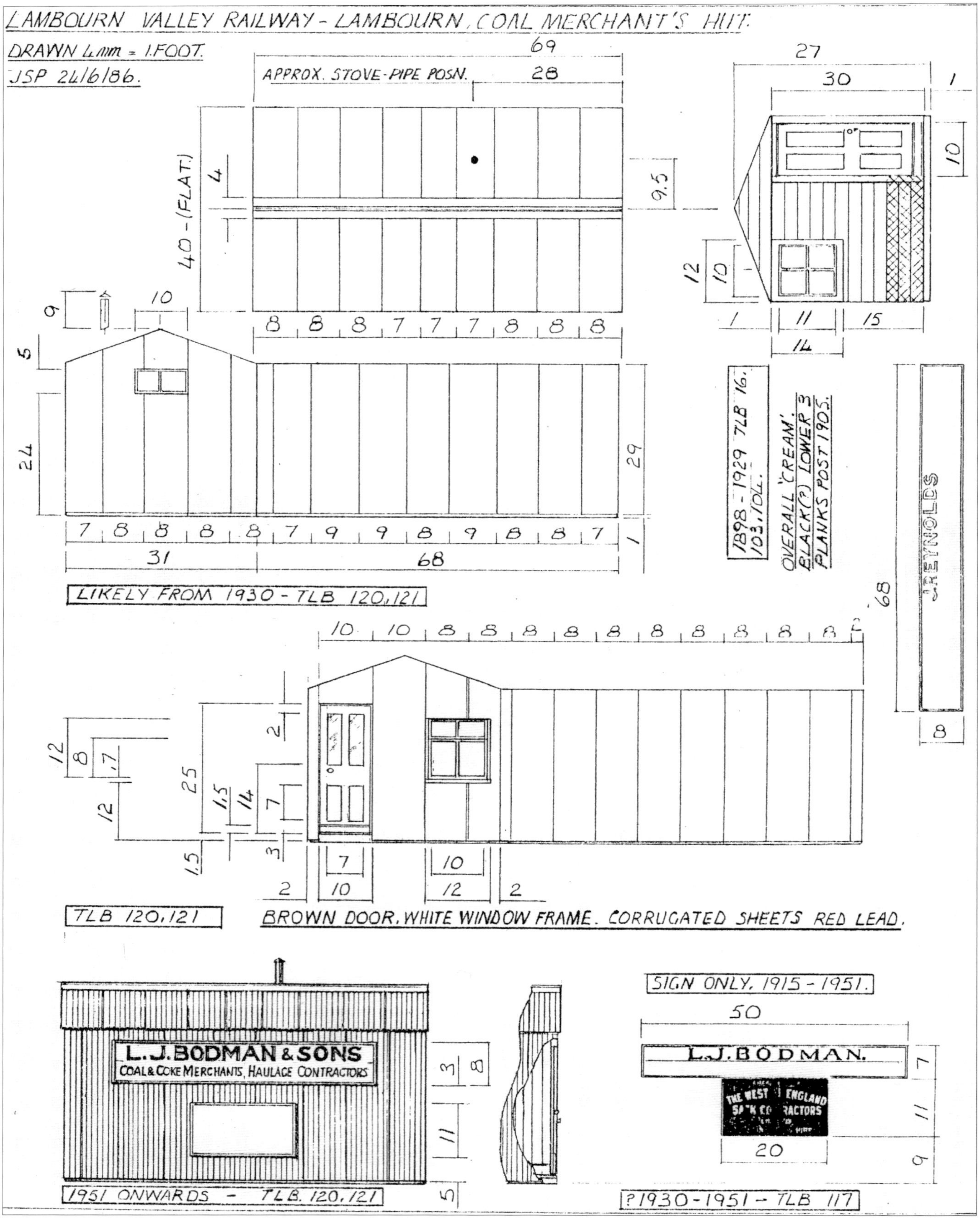

LAMBOURN VALLEY RAILWAY - LAMBOURN, COAL MERCHANT'S HUT.

DRAWN 4mm = 1 FOOT.
JSP 24/6/86.

APPROX. STOVE-PIPE POSN.

69
28

27
30
1

40 - (FLAT.)

8 8 8 7 7 7 8 8 8

9.5
10
12 10
1 11 15
14

1898 - 1929 TLB. 16.
103, 104.

OVERALL 'CREAM'.
BLACK(?) LOWER 3
PLANKS POST 1905.

5
9 10
24
31
7 8 8 8 8 7 9 9 8 9 8 8 7 1
68
29

LIKELY FROM 1930 - TLB 120, 121

J. REYNOLDS

68
8

10 10 8 8 8 8 8 8 8 8 8 8

12 8 7
25 15 14 7
12
1.5 3
2 10
7 10 12 2

TLB 120, 121   BROWN DOOR, WHITE WINDOW FRAME. CORRUGATED SHEETS RED LEAD.

L.J. BODMAN & SONS
COAL & COKE MERCHANTS, HAULAGE CONTRACTORS

3 8
11
5

1951 ONWARDS - TLB. 120, 121

SIGN ONLY. 1915 - 1951.
50
L.J. BODMAN.
7
THE WEST ENGLAND
SACK CONTRACTORS
20
11 9

?1930 - 1951 - TLB 117

124

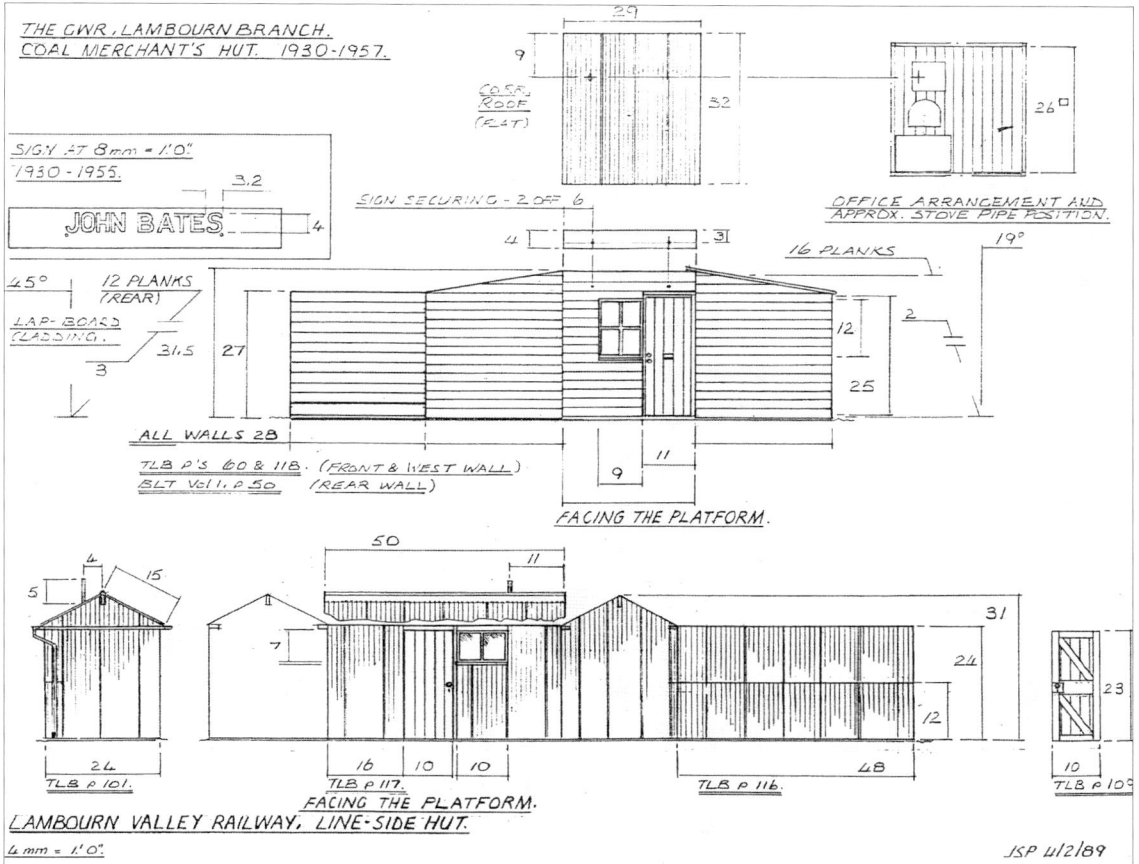

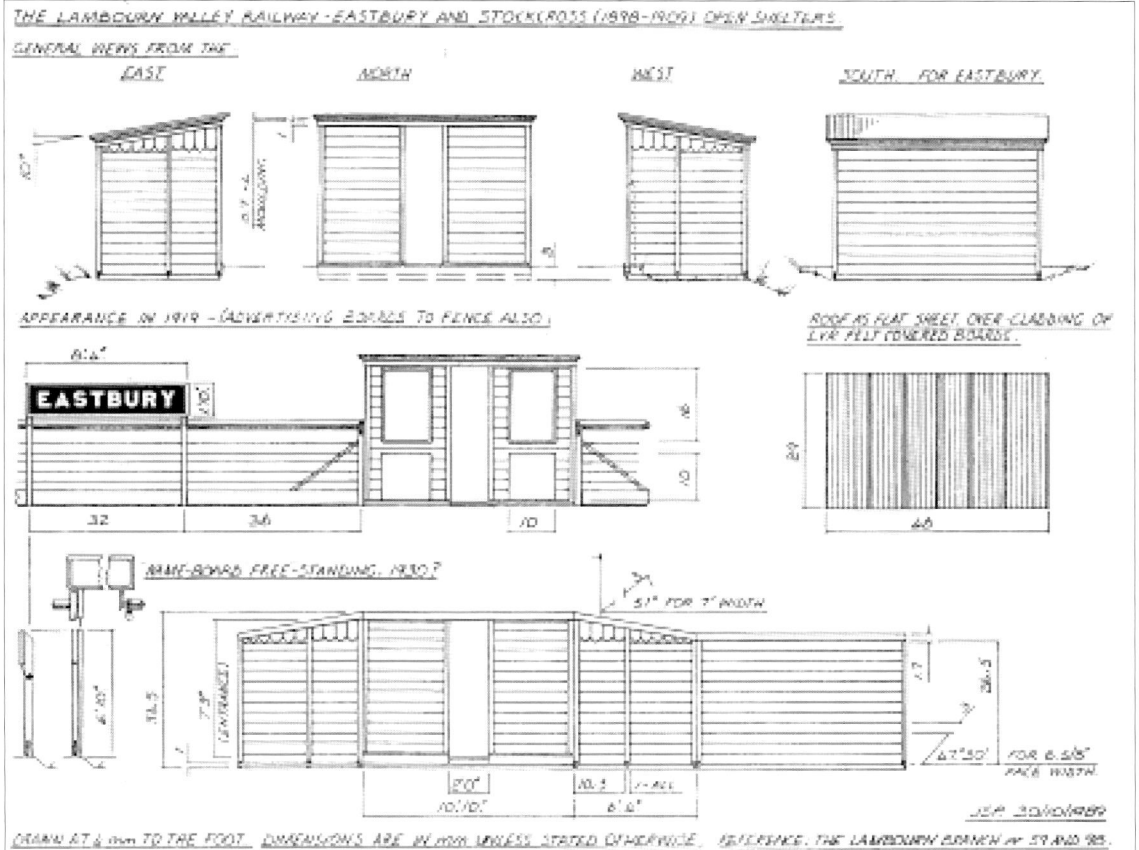

THE GWR, LAMBOURN BRANCH.
COAL MERCHANT'S HUT. 1930-1957.

SIGN AT 8mm = 1'0".
1930 - 1955.

JOHN BATES

FACING THE PLATFORM.

LAMBOURN VALLEY RAILWAY, LINE-SIDE HUT.

THE LAMBOURN VALLEY RAILWAY - EASTBURY AND STOCKCROSS (1898-1906) OPEN SHELTERS

EASTBURY

125

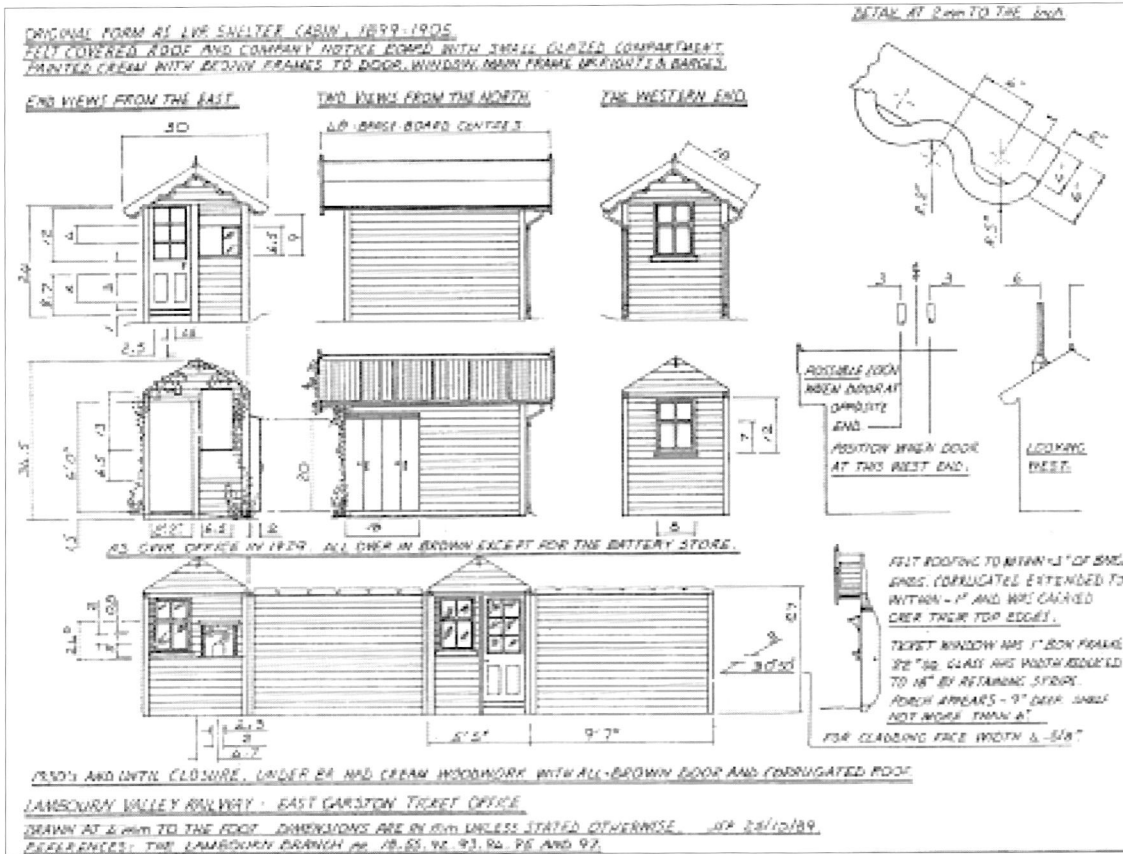

Opposite page - The classic view of the terminus, probably soon after nationalisation.

Two members of staff, not identified, stand facing the camera, whilst the garden, referred to by David Rosier, can be seen either side of the platform seat. (It is not known if Lambourn was ever awarded a prize in the GWR and later BR annual 'Station Gardens' competitions). The scene had altered little over the years, cosmetic alterations yes, but apart from the removal of the engine shed and diesel railcar the scene could be almost anytime between 1910 and 1960.

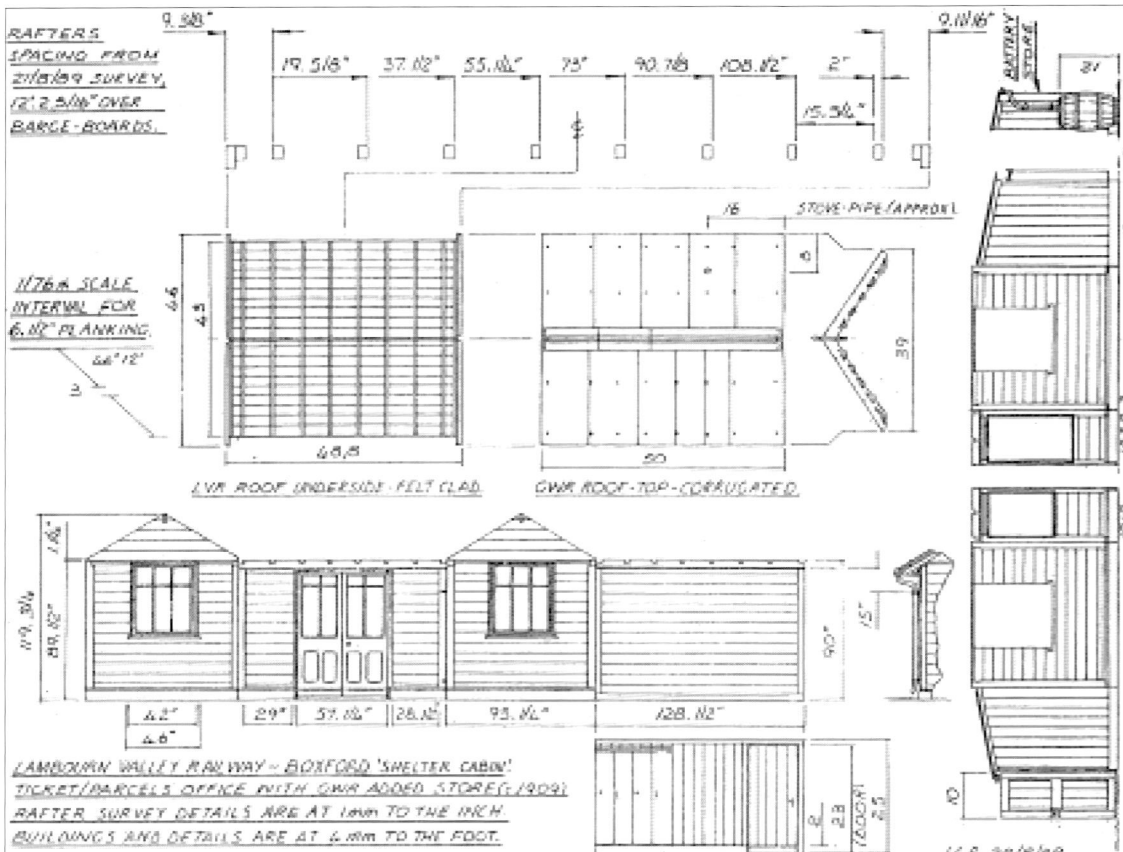

FRONT (PLATFORM) VIEW. APPEARANCE UNTIL 1957 (CARRIER).

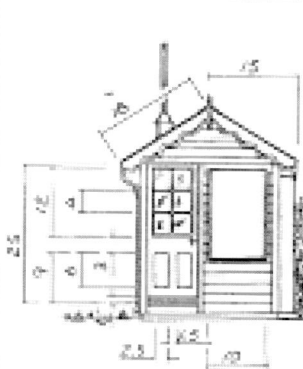

VIEW FROM THE WEST WITH CENTRAL RAILWAY STORE.

REAR VIEW. SHOWING ORIGINAL FALL PIPES POSN.

PLATFORM APPROACH (EAST) VIEW. APPEARANCE IN 1919 POSSIBLY UNTIL 1950. AB - BARGE-BOARD CENTRES.

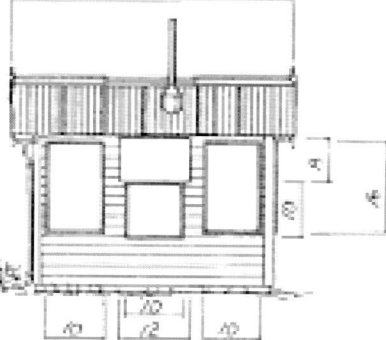

SPARS CENTRES.

REPLACEMENT PLAIN CLADDING - 1959.

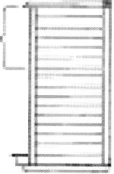

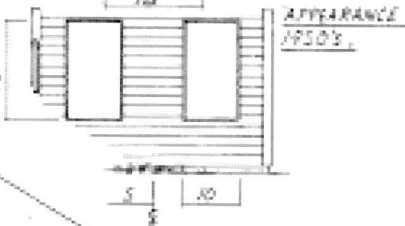

APPEARANCE 1950's

LAMBOURN VALLEY RAILWAY- SPEEN TICKET OFFICE. DRAWN AT 4 mm TO THE FOOT. JSP 28/10/89. DIMENSIONS ARE IN mm UNLESS STATED OTHERWISE. REFERENCE: THE LAMBOURN BRANCH pp 18, 72 AND 97.

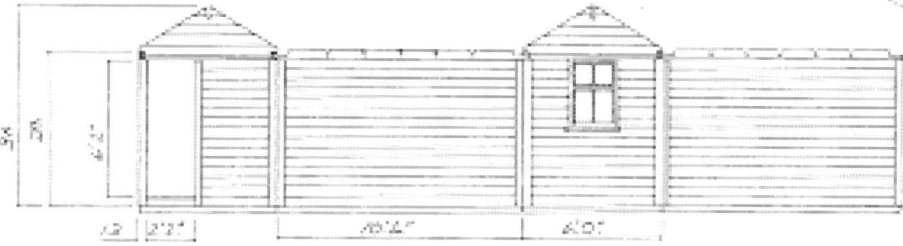

BARGE-BOARD RECONSTRUCTION AT 2 mm x 1 inch BASED ON THE FULL FRONT-FACE VIEW OF THE IDENTICAL FITTING AT EAST CAPSTONE.

Final sad comparisons. From working railway to desolation and abandonment, the only feet now walking the platform that of the vandals. The Lambourn branch served its community well, it provided employment and a way of life to successive generations. Today it may be just the memories that remain, but these should not be allowed to be forgotten.

ADDENDA TO THE ORIGINAL WORK

Peter Penfold has kindly provided details of comments made by his father, the late John Penfold, appertaining to the original work. These are quoted verbatim. The page numbers shown refer to the original book.

Page 36	There was a bookmaker in Lambourn who took all the bets from the station (including the Station Master's).
Page 47	Clerks did not remove money from the till! The District Auditor arrived unheralded, unless one of the men further down the line happened to recognise him.
Page 107	The Carting agent was Albert Bracey with horse and cart. His son, also Albert, owned the motor lorries which he used to collect horse manure from the stables and forwarded it to various destinations for mushroom growing. Albert (senior) ceased to be captain of the Fire Brigade in 1930 when a new motor engine took over.
Page 112	The unknown lady is Miss Hunt. (Later Mrs Horsely). The lad in the back row is not Bob Sampson.

For the concluding scene, what better way than Bernard Smith leaving Welford Park for Newbury at the end of the shift. It was whilst returning home to Newbury one day on what was the original B4000 running through Boxford and Speen, that Bernard was in collision with a vehicle coming at him on the wrong side of the road. The resultant collision left him with a fractured leg in the roadway, the offending driver having checked to see he was still alive, drove off. Bernard recall's his main fear was of being run over by another vehicle approaching as, understandably, he was unable to move. The offending driver also suspected of being inebriated. Fortunately another motorist came upon the scene and used his own vehicle to protect the injured Bernard until an ambulance arrived. He was off work for a year, but returned later to continue his life as a signalman at Welford Park.